Edmund Gosse, Edmund Henry Garrett

Victorian Songs

Lyrics of the Affections and Nature

Edmund Gosse, Edmund Henry Garrett

Victorian Songs
Lyrics of the Affections and Nature

ISBN/EAN: 9783744774444

Printed in Europe, USA, Canada, Australia, Japan

Cover: Foto ©Thomas Meinert / pixelio.de

More available books at **www.hansebooks.com**

Victorian Songs
Lyrics of the Affections and Nature

Collected and Illustrated by Edmund H. Garrett with an Introduction by Edmund Gosse

Little Brown and Company
Boston

Ingelow; to Messrs. Stone & Kimball, for songs by Norman Gale; to Messrs. Dodd, Mead & Co., for the use of poems by Austin Dobson; to Messrs. Roberts Brothers, for songs by F. W. Bourdillon, Jean Ingelow, and Sir Edwin Arnold; and to Lord Dufferin, for permission to include poems by Lady Dufferin.

He also gratefully acknowledges the permission to include their poems extended to him by the following authors: Austin Dobson, Hamilton Aïdé, Aubrey de Vere, Joseph Skipsey, Sir Edwin Arnold, Norman Gale, Michael Field, F. W. Bourdillon, and the late Sir Frederick Locker-Lampson; and to Edmund Gosse, who kindly consented to write the Introduction.

CONTENTS

Where are the songs I used to know?

CHRISTINA ROSSETTI.

Contents.

Contents.

Contents.

An Index to First Lines

Listen — Songs thou 'lt hear
Through the wide world ringing.

BARRY CORNWALL.

Victorian Songs.

Index to First Lines.

Index to First Lines.

LIST OF ILLUSTRATIONS

INTRODUCTION

> The writer of prose, by intelligence taught,
> Says the thing that will please, in the way that he ought.
>
> FREDERICK LOCKER-LAMPSON.

NO species of poetry is more ancient than the lyrical, and yet none shows so little sign of having outlived the requirements of human passion. The world may grow tired of epics and of tragedies, but each generation, as it sees the hawthorns blossom and the freshness of girlhood ex-

pand, is seized with a pang which nothing but the spasm of verse will relieve. Each youth imagines that spring-tide and love are wonders which he is the first of human beings to appreciate, and he burns to alleviate his emotion in rhyme. Historians exaggerate, perhaps, the function of music in awakening and guiding the exercise of lyrical poetry. The lyric exists, they tell us, as an accompaniment to the lyre; and without the mechanical harmony the spoken song is an artifice. Quite as plausibly might it be avowed that music was but added to verse to concentrate and emphasize its rapture, to add poignancy and volume to its expression. But the truth is that these two arts, though sometimes happily allied, are, and always have been, independent. When verse has been innocent enough to lean on music, we may be likely to find that music also has been of the simplest order, and that the pair of them, like two delicious children, have tottered and swayed together down the flowery meadows of experience. When either poetry or music is adult, the presence of each is a distrac-

tion to the other, and each prefers, in the elaborate ages, to stand alone, since the mystery of the one confounds the complexity of the other. Most poets hate music; few musicians comprehend the nature of poetry; and the combination of these arts has probably, in all ages, been contrived, not for the satisfaction of artists, but for the convenience of their public.

This divorce between poetry and music has been more frankly accepted in the present century than ever before, and is nowadays scarcely opposed in serious criticism. If music were a necessary ornament of lyrical verse, the latter would nowadays scarcely exist; but we hear less and less of the poet's devotion (save in a purely conventional sense) to the lute and the pipe. What we call the Victorian lyric is absolutely independent of any such aid. It may be that certain songs of Tennyson and Christina Rossetti have been with great popularity "set," as it is called, "to music." So far as the latter is in itself successful, it stultifies the former; and we admit at last that the idea of one art aiding another in this combination is absolutely fictitious. The beauty—even the beauty of sound—conveyed by the ear in such lyrics as "Break, break, break," or "When I am dead, my dearest," is obscured, is exchanged for another and a rival species of beauty, by the most exquisite musical setting that a composer can invent.

The age which has been the first to accept this condition, then, should be rich in frankly lyrical poetry; and this we find to be the case with the Victorian period. At no time has a greater mass of this species of verse been produced, not even in the combined Elizabethan and Jacobean age. But when we come to consider the quality of this later harvest of song, we observe in it a far less homogeneous character. We can take a piece of verse, and decide at sight that it must be Elizabethan, or of the age of the Pléiade in France, or of a particular period in Italy. Even an ode of our own eighteenth century is hardly to be confounded with a fragment from any other school. The great Georgian age introduced a wide variety into English poetry; and yet we have but to examine the selected jewels strung into so exquisite a carcanet by Mr. Palgrave in his "Golden Treasury" to notice with surprise how close a family likeness exists between the contributions of Shelley, Wordsworth, Keats, and Byron. The distinctions of style, of course, are very great; but the general character of the diction, the imagery, even of the rhythm, is more or less identical. The stamp of the same age is upon them,—they are hall-marked 1820.

It is perhaps too early to decide that this will never be the case with the Victorian lyrics. While we live in an age we see the distinction of its parts, rather than their co-relation. It is said that the Japanese Government once sent over a Commission to report upon the art of Europe; and that, having visited the exhibitions of London, Paris, Florence, and Berlin, the Commissioners confessed that the works of the European painters all looked so exactly alike that it was difficult to distinguish one from another. The Japanese eye, trained in absolutely opposed conventions, could not tell the difference between a Watts and a Fortuny, a Théodore Rousseau and a Henry Moore. So it is quite possible, it is even probable, that future critics may see a close similarity where we see nothing but divergence between the various productions of the Victorian age. Yet we can judge but what we discern; and certainly to the critical eye to-day it is the absence of a central tendency, the chaotic cultivation of all contrivable varieties of style, which most strikingly seems to distinguish the times we live in.

We use the word "Victorian" in literature to distinguish what was written after the decline of that age of which Walter Scott, Coleridge, and Wordsworth were the survivors. It is well to recollect, however, that Tennyson, who is the Victorian writer par excellence, *had published the most individual and characteristic of his lyrics long before the Queen ascended the throne, and that Elizabeth Barrett, Henry Taylor, William Barnes, and others were by this date of mature age. It is difficult to remind ourselves, who have lived in the radiance of that august figure, that some of the most beautiful of Tenny-*

son's lyrics, such as "Mariana" and "The Dying Swan," are now separated from us by as long a period of years as divided them from Dr. Johnson and the author of "Night Thoughts." The reflection is of value only as warning us of the extraordinary length of the epoch we still call "Victorian." It covers, not a mere generation, but much more than half a century. During this length of time a complete revolution in literary taste might have been expected to take place. This has not occurred, and the cause may very well be the extreme license permitted to the poets to adopt whatever style they pleased. Where all the doors stand wide open, there is no object in escaping; where there is but one door, and that one barred, it is human nature to fret for some violent means of evasion. How divine have been the methods of the Victorian lyrists may easily be exemplified:—

> *"Quoth tongue of neither maid nor wife*
> *To heart of neither wife nor maid,*
> *Lead we not here a jolly life*
> *Betwixt the shine and shade?*

> *"Quoth heart of neither maid nor wife*
> *To tongue of neither wife nor maid,*
> *Thou wagg'st, but I am worn with strife,*
> *And feel like flowers that fade."*

That is a masterpiece, but so is this:—

> *"Nay, but you who do not love her,*
> *Is she not pure gold, my mistress?*
> *Holds earth aught—speak truth—above her?*
> *Aught like this tress, see, and this tress,*
> *And this last fairest tress of all,*
> *—So fair, see, ere I let it fall?*
>
> *"Because, you spend your lives in praisings,*
> *To praise, you search the wide world over:*
> *Then why not witness, calmly gazing,*
> *If earth holds aught—speak truth—above her?*
> *Above this tress, and this I touch,*
> *But cannot praise, I love so much!"*

And so is this:—

> *"Under the wide and starry sky,*
> *Dig the grave and let me lie.*
> *Glad did I live and gladly die,*
> *And I laid me down with a will.*

"*This be the verse you grave for me:*
Here he lies where he longed to be;
Home is the sailor, home from sea,
And the hunter home from the hill."

But who would believe that the writers of these were contemporaries?

If we examine more closely the forms which lyric poetry has taken since 1830, *we shall find that certain influences at work in the minds of our leading writers have led to the widest divergence in the character of lyrical verse. It will be well, perhaps, to consider in turn the leading classes of that work. It was not to be expected that in an age of such complexity and self-consciousness as ours, the pure song, the simple trill of bird-like melody, should often or prominently be heard. As civilization spreads, it ceases to be possible, or at least it becomes less and less usual, that simple emotion should express itself with absolute naïveté. Perhaps Burns was the latest poet in these islands whose passion warbled forth in perfectly artless strains; and he had the advantage of using a dialect still unsubdued and unvulgarized. Artlessness nowadays must be the result of the most exquisitely finished art; if not, it is apt to be insipid, if not positively squalid and fusty. The obvious uses of simple words have been exhausted; we cannot, save by infinite pains and the exercise of a happy genius, recover the old spontaneous air, the effect of an inevitable arrangement of the only possible words.*

This beautiful direct simplicity, however, was not infrequently secured by Tennyson, and scarcely less often by Christina Rossetti, both of whom have left behind them jets of pure emotional melody which compare to advantage with the most perfect specimens of Greek and Elizabethan song. Tennyson did not very often essay this class of writing, but when he did, he rarely failed; his songs combine, with extreme naturalness and something of a familiar sweetness, a felicity of workmanship hardly to be excelled. In her best songs, Miss Rossetti is scarcely, if at all, his inferior; but her judgment was far less sure, and she was more ready to look with complacency on her failures. The songs of Mr. Aubrey de were are not well enough known; they are sometimes singularly charming. Other poets have once or twice succeeded in catching this clear natural treble,—the living linnet once captured in the elm, as Tusitala puts it; but this has not been a gift largely enjoyed by our Victorian poets.

The richer and more elaborate forms of lyric, on the contrary, have exactly suited this curious and learned age of ours. The species of verse which, originally Italian or French, have now so abundantly and so admirably been practised in England that we can no longer think of them as exotic, having found so many exponents in the Victorian period that they are pre-eminently characteristic of it. "Scorn not the Sonnet," said Wordsworth to his contemporaries; but the lesson has not been needed in the second half of the century. The sonnet is the most solid and unsingable of the sections of lyrical poetry; it is difficult to think of it as chanted to a musical accompaniment. It is used with great distinction by writers to whom skill in the lighter divisions of poetry has been denied, and there are poets, such as Bowles and Charles Tennyson-Turner, who live by their sonnets alone. The practice of the sonnet has been so extended that all sense of monotony has been lost. A sonnet by Elizabeth Barrett Browning differs from one by D. G. Rossetti or by Matthew Arnold to such excess as to make it difficult for us to realize that the form in each case is absolutely identical.

With the sonnet might be mentioned the lighter forms of elaborate exotic verse; but to these a word shall be given later on. More closely allied to the sonnet are those rich and somewhat fantastic stanza-measures in which Rossetti delighted. Those in which Keats and the Italians have each their part have been greatly used by the Victorian poets. They lend themselves to a melancholy magnificence, to pomp of movement and gorgeousness of color; the very sight of them gives the page the look of an ancient blazoned window. Poems of this class are "The Stream's Secret" and the choruses in "Love is enough." They satisfy the appetite of our time for subtle and vague analysis of emotion, for what appeals to the spirit through the senses; but here, again, in different hands, the "thing," the metrical instrument, takes wholly diverse characters, and we seek in vain for a formula that can include Robert Browning and Gabriel Rossetti, William Barnes and Arthur Hugh Clough.

From this highly elaborated and extended species of lyric the transition is easy to the Ode. In the Victorian age, the ode, in its full Pindaric sense, has not been very frequently used. We have specimens by Mr. Swinburne in which the Dorian laws are closely adhered to. But the ode, in a more or less irregular form, whether pæan or threnody, has been the instrument of several of our leading lyrists. The genius of Mr. Swinburne, even to a greater degree than that of Shelley, is essentially dithyrambic, and is never happier than when it spreads its wings as wide as those of the wild swan, and soars upon the very breast of tempest. In these flights Mr. Swinburne attains to a volume of sonorous melody such as no other poet, perhaps, of the world has reached, and we may say to him, as he has shouted to the Mater Triumphalis :—

> *" Darkness to daylight shall lift up thy pæan,*
> *Hill to hill thunder, vale cry back to vale,*
> *With wind-notes as of eagles Æschylean,*
> *And Sappho singing in the nightingale."*

Nothing could mark more picturesquely the wide diversity permitted in Victorian lyric than to turn from the sonorous and tumultuous odes of Mr. Swinburne to those of Mr. Patmore, in which stateliness of contemplation and a peculiar austerity of tenderness find their expression in odes of iambic cadence, the melody of which depends, not in their headlong torrent of sound, but in the cunning variation of catalectic pause. A similar form has been adopted by Lord De Tabley for many of his gorgeous studies of antique myth, and by Tennyson for his " Death of the Duke of Wellington." It is an error to call these iambic odes " irregular," although they do not follow the classic rules with strophe, antistrophe, and epode. The enchanting " I have led her home," in

"Maud," is an example of this kind of lyric at its highest point of perfection.

A branch of lyrical poetry which has been very widely cultivated in the Victorian age is the philosophical, or gnomic, in which a serious chain of thought, often illustrated by complex and various imagery, is held in a casket of melodious verse, elaborately rhymed. Matthew Arnold was a master of this kind of poetry, which takes its form, through Wordsworth, from the solemn and so-called "metaphysical" writers of the seventeenth century. We class this interesting and abundant section of verse with the lyrical, because we know not by what other name to describe it; yet it has obviously as little as possible of the singing ecstasy about it. It neither pours its heart out in a rapture, nor wails forth its despair. It has as little of the nightingale's rich melancholy as of the lark's delirium. It hardly sings, but, with infinite decorum and sobriety, speaks its melodious message to mankind. This sort of philosophical poetry is really critical; its function is to analyze and describe; and it ap-

proaches, save for the enchantment of its form, nearer to prose than do the other sections of the art. It is, however, just this species of poetry which has particularly appealed to the age in which we live; and how naturally it does so may be seen in the welcome extended to the polished and serene compositions of Mr. William Watson.

Almost a creation, or at least a complete conquest, of the Victorian age is the humorous lyric in its more delicate developments. If the past can point to Prior and to Praed, we can boast, in their various departments, of Calverly, of Locker-Lampson, of Mr. Andrew Lang, of Mr. W. S. Gilbert. The comic muse, indeed, has marvellously extended her blandishments during the last two generations, and has discovered methods of trivial elegance which were quite unknown to our forefathers. Here must certainly be said a word in favor of those French forms of verse, all essentially lyrical, such as the ballad, the rondel, the triolet, which have been used so abundantly as to become quite a feature in our lighter literature. These are not, or are but rarely, fitted to bear the burden of high emotion; but their precision, and the deftness which their use demands fit them exceedingly well for the more distinguished kind of persiflage. No one has kept these delicate butterflies in flight with the agile movement of his fan so admirably as Mr. Austin Dobson, that neatest of magicians.

Those who write hastily of Victorian lyrical poetry are apt to find fault with its lack of spontaneity. It is true that we cannot pretend to discover on a greensward so often crossed and re-crossed as the poetic language of England many morning dewdrops still glistening on the grasses. We have to pay the penalty of our experience in a certain lack of innocence. The artless graces of a child seem mincing affectations in a grown-up woman. But the poetry of this age has amply made up for any lack of innocence by its sumptuous fulness, its variety, its magnificent accomplishment, its felicitous response to a multitude of moods and apprehen-

sions. It has struck out no new field for itself; it still remains where the romantic revolution of 1798 *placed it; its aims are not other than were those of Coleridge and of Keats. But within that defined sphere it has developed a surprising activity. It has occupied the attention and become the facile instrument of men of the greatest genius, writers of whom any age and any language might be proud. It has been tender and fiery, severe and voluminous, gorgeous and marmoreal, in turns. It has translated into words feelings so subtle, so transitory, moods so fragile and intangible, that the rough hand of prose would but have crushed them. And this, surely, indicates the great gift of Victorian lyrical poetry to the race. During a time of extreme mental and moral restlessness, a time of speculation and evolution, when all illusions are tested, all conventions overthrown, when the harder elements of life have been brought violently to the front, and where there is a temptation for the emancipated mind roughly to reject what is not material and obvious, this art has preserved intact the lovelier delusions of the spirit, all that is vague and incorporeal and illusory. So that for Victorian Lyric generally no better final definition can be given than is supplied by Mr. Robert Bridges in a little poem of incomparable beauty, which may fitly bring this essay to a close:—*

"I have loved flowers that fade,
Within whose magic tents
Rich hues have marriage made
With sweet immemorial scents:
A joy of love at sight,—
A honeymoon delight,
That ages in an hour:—
My song be like a flower.

"I have loved airs that die
Before their charm is writ
Upon the liquid sky
Trembling to welcome it.
Notes that with pulse of fire
Proclaim the spirit's desire,
Then die, and are nowhere:—
My song be like an air."

EDMUND GOSSE.

Victorian · Songs

"Short swallow-flights of song"

TENNYSON

HAMILTON AÏDÉ.

1830.

REMEMBER OR FORGET.

I.

I SAT beside the streamlet,
  I watched the water flow,
As we together watched it
  One little year ago;
The soft rain pattered on the leaves,
  The April grass was wet,
Ah! folly to remember;—
  'Tis wiser to forget.

II.

The nightingales made vocal
  June's palace paved with gold;
I watched the rose you gave me
  Its warm red heart unfold;
But breath of rose and bird's song
  Were fraught with wild regret.
'T is madness to remember;
  'T were wisdom to forget.

III.

I stood among the gold corn,
  Alas! no more, I knew,
To gather gleaner's measure
  Of the love that fell from you.
For me, no gracious harvest—
  Would God we ne'er had met!
'T is hard, Love, to remember, but
  'T is harder to forget.

IV.

The streamlet now is frozen,
  The nightingales are fled,

Hamilton Aïdé.

The cornfields are deserted,
  And every rose is dead.
I sit beside my lonely fire,
  And pray for wisdom yet—
For calmness to remember
  Or courage to forget.

OH, LET ME DREAM.

FROM "A NINE DAYS' WONDER."

OH! let me dream of happy days gone by,
Forgetting sorrows that have come between,
As sunlight gilds some distant summit high,
And leaves the valleys dark that intervene.
The phantoms of remorse that haunt
The soul, are laid beneath that spell;
As, in the music of a chaunt
Is lost the tolling of a bell.
Oh! let me dream of happy days gone by, etc.

In youth, we plucked full many a flower that died,
Dropped on the pathway, as we danced along;
And now, we cherish each poor leaflet dried
In pages which to that dear past belong.
With sad crushed hearts they yet retain
Some semblance of their glories fled;
Like us, whose lineaments remain,
When all the fires of life are dead.
Oh! let me dream, etc.

LOVE, THE PILGRIM.

SUGGESTED BY A SKETCH BY E. BURNE-JONES.

EVERY day a Pilgrim, blindfold,
When the night and morning meet,
Entereth the slumbering city,
Stealeth down the silent street;
Lingereth round some battered doorway,
Leaves unblest some portal grand,
And the walls, where sleep the children,
Toucheth, with his warm young hand.
Love is passing! Love is passing!—
Passing while ye lie asleep:
In your blessèd dreams, O children,
Give him all your hearts to keep!

Blindfold is this Pilgrim, Maiden.
Though to-day he touched thy door,
He may pass it by to-morrow—
—Pass it—to return no more.

Let us then with prayers entreat him,—
  Youth! her heart, whose coldness grieves,
May one morn by Love be softened;
  Prize the treasure that he leaves.
    Love is passing! Love is passing!
      All, with hearts to hope and pray,
    Bid this pilgrim touch the lintels
      Of your doorways every day.

WILLIAM ALLINGHAM.

1824-1889.

LOVELY MARY DONNELLY.

OH, lovely Mary Donnelly, my joy, my only best!
If fifty girls were round you, I 'd hardly see the rest;
Be what it may the time o' day, the place be where it will,
Sweet looks o' Mary Donnelly, they bloom before me still.

Her eyes like mountain water that 's flowing on a rock,
How clear they are, how dark they are! they give me many a shock;
Red rowans warm in sunshine and wetted with a show'r,
Could ne'er express the charming lip that has me in its pow'r.

Her nose is straight and handsome, her eyebrows
lifted up,
Her chin is very neat and pert, and smooth like a
china cup,
Her hair's the brag of Ireland, so weighty and so
fine;
It's rolling down upon her neck, and gathered in a twine.

The dance o' last Whit-Monday night exceeded all
before,
No pretty girl for miles about was missing from the
floor;
But Mary kept the belt o' love, and O but she was gay!
She danced a jig, she sung a song, that took my
heart away.

When she stood up for dancing, her steps were so
complete
The music nearly kill'd itself to listen to her feet;
The fiddler moaned his blindness, he heard her so
much praised,
But bless'd his luck to not be deaf when once her
voice she raised.

And evermore I 'm whistling or lilting what you sung,
Your smile is always in my heart, your name beside
my tongue ;
But you 've as many sweethearts as you 'd count on
both your hands,
And for myself there 's not a thumb or little finger
stands.

'T is you 're the flower o' womankind in country or in
town ;
The higher I exalt you, the lower I 'm cast down.
If some great lord should come this way, and see
your beauty bright,
And you to be his lady, I 'd own it was but right.

O might we live together in a lofty palace hall,
Where joyful music rises, and where scarlet curtains
fall !
O might we live together in a cottage mean and
small,
With sods o' grass the only roof, and mud the only
wall !

O lovely Mary Donnelly, your beauty 's my distress.
It 's far too beauteous to be mine, but I 'll never wish it less.
The proudest place would fit your face, and I am poor and low;
But blessings be about you, dear, wherever you may go!

SONG.

O SPIRIT of the Summertime!
Bring back the roses to the dells;
The swallow from her distant clime,
The honey-bee from drowsy cells.

Bring back the friendship of the sun;
The gilded evenings, calm and late,
When merry children homeward run,
And peeping stars bid lovers wait.

Bring back the singing; and the scent
Of meadowlands at dewy prime;—
Oh, bring again my heart's content,
Thou Spirit of the Summertime!

SERENADE.

OH, hearing sleep, and sleeping hear,
The while we dare to call thee dear,
So may thy dreams be good, altho'
The loving power thou dost not know.
As music parts the silence, — lo!
Through heaven the stars begin to peep,
To comfort us that darkling pine
Because those fairer lights of thine
Have set into the Sea of Sleep.
Yet closèd still thine eyelids keep;
And may our voices through the sphere
Of Dreamland all as softly rise
As through these shadowy rural dells,
Where bashful Echo somewhere dwells,
And touch thy spirit to as soft replies.
May peace from gentle guardian skies,
Till watches of the dark are worn,
Surround thy bed, and joyous morn

Makes all the chamber rosy bright!
Good-night!—From far-off fields is borne
The drowsy Echo's faint 'Good-night,'—
Good-night! Good-night!

ACROSS THE SEA.

I WALKED in the lonesome evening,
And who so sad as I,
When I saw the young men and maidens
Merrily passing by.
To thee, my Love, to thee —
So fain would I come to thee!
While the ripples fold upon sands of gold,
And I look across the sea.

I stretch out my hands; who will clasp them?
I call, — thou repliest no word.
Oh, why should heart-longing be weaker
Than the waving wings of a bird!
To thee, my Love, to thee —
So fain would I come to thee!
For the tide 's at rest from east to west,
And I look across the sea.

Across the Sea

There 's joy in the hopeful morning,
  There 's peace in the parting day,
There 's sorrow with every lover
  Whose true love is far away.
    To thee, my Love, to thee —
    So fain would I come to thee!
And the water 's bright in a still moonlight,
    As I look across the sea.

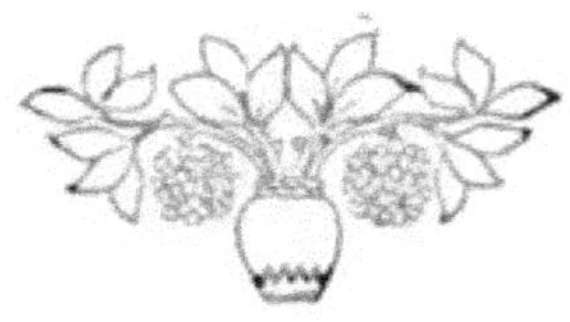

SIR EDWIN ARNOLD.

1832.

SERENADE.

LUTE! breathe thy lowest in my Lady's ear,
  Sing while she sleeps, "Ah! belle dame, aimez-
    vous?"
Till, dreaming still, she dream that I am here,
  And wake to find it, as my love is, true;
Then, when she listens in her warm white nest,
  Say in slow music, — softer, tenderer yet,
That lute-strings quiver when their tone 's at rest,
  And my heart trembles when my lips are set.

Stars! if my sweet love still a-dreaming lies,
  Shine through the roses for a lover's sake
And send your silver to her lidded eyes,
  Kissing them very gently till she wake;

Then while she wonders at the lay and light,
    Tell her, though morning endeth star and song,
That ye live still, when no star glitters bright,
    And my love lasteth, though it finds no tongue.

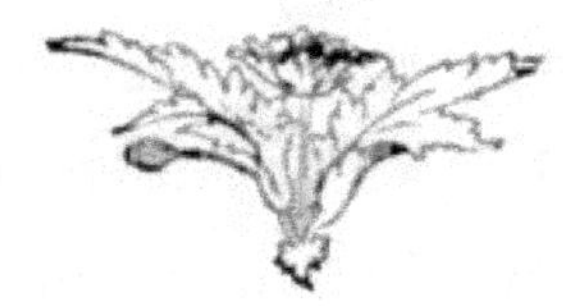

A LOVE SONG OF HENRI QUATRE.

COME, rosy Day!
Come quick — I pray —
I am so glad when I thee see!
Because my Fair,
Who is so dear,
Is rosy-red and white like thee.

She lives, I think,
On heavenly drink
Dawn-dew, which Hebe pours for her;
Else — when I sip
At her soft lip
How smells it of ambrosia?

She is so fair
None can compare;
And, oh, her slender waist divine!
Her sparkling eyes
Set in the skies
The morning stars would far outshine!

Only to hear
Her voice so clear
The village gathers in the street;
And Tityrus,
Grown one of us,
Leaves piping on his flute so sweet.

The Graces three,
Where'er she be,
Call all the Loves to flutter nigh;
And what she'll say, —
Speak when she may, —
Is full of sense and majesty!

THOMAS ASHE.

1836-1889.

NO AND YES.

IF I could choose my paradise,
  And please myself with choice of bliss,
Then I would have your soft blue eyes
  And rosy little mouth to kiss!
Your lips, as smooth and tender, child,
As rose-leaves in a coppice wild.

If fate bade choose some sweet unrest,
  To weave my troubled life a snare,
Then I would say "her maiden breast
  And golden ripple of her hair;"
And weep amid those tresses, child,
Contented to be thus beguiled.

AT ALTENAHR.

1872.

Meet we no angels, Pansie?

CAME, on a Sabbath noon, my sweet,
In white, to find her lover;
The grass grew proud beneath her feet,
The green elm-leaves above her: —
Meet we no angels, Pansie?

She said, "We meet no angels now;"
And soft lights streamed upon her;
And with white hand she touched a bough;
She did it that great honour: —
What! meet no angels, Pansie?

O sweet brown hat, brown hair, brown eyes
Down-dropped brown eyes so tender!
Then what said I? — Gallant replies
Seem flattery, and offend her: —
But, — meet no angels, Pansie?

MARIT.

1869-70.

C'est un songe que d'y penser.

MY love, on a fair May morning,
  Would weave a garland of May:
The dew hung frore, as her foot tripped o'er
  The grass at dawn of the day;
On leaf and stalk, in each green wood-walk,
  Till the sun should charm it away.

Green as a leaf her kirtle,
  Her bodice red as a rose:
Her white bare feet went softly and sweet
  By roots where the violet grows;
Where speedwells azure as heaven,
  Their sleepy eyes half close.

O'er arms as fair as the lilies
  No sleeve my love drew on:
She found a bower of the wildrose flower,
  And for her breast culled one:
And I laugh and know her breasts will grow
  Or ever a year be gone.

O sweet dream, wrought of a dear fore-thought,
  Of a golden time to fall!
She seemed to sing, in her wandering,
  Till doves in the elm-tops tall
Grew mute to hear; as her song rang clear
  How love is the lord of all.

ALFRED AUSTIN.

1835.

A NIGHT IN JUNE.

LADY! in this night of June,
 Fair like thee and holy,
Art thou gazing at the moon
 That is rising slowly?
  I am gazing on her now:
  Something tells me, so art thou.

Night hath been when thou and I
 Side by side were sitting,
Watching o'er the moonlit sky
 Fleecy cloudlets flitting.
  Close our hands were linkèd then;
  When will they be linked again?

What to me the starlight still,
  Or the moonbeams' splendour,
If I do not feel the thrill
  Of thy fingers slender?
    Summer nights in vain are clear,
    If thy footstep be not near.

Roses slumbering in their sheaths
  O'er my threshold clamber,
And the honeysuckle wreathes
  Its translucent amber
    Round the gables of my home:
    How is it thou dost not come?

If thou camest, rose on rose
  From its sleep would waken;
From each flower and leaf that blows
  Spices would be shaken;
    Floating down from star and tree,
    Dreamy perfumes welcome thee.

I would lead thee where the leaves
  In the moon-rays glisten;
And, where shadows fall in sheaves,
  We would lean and listen
    For the song of that sweet bird
    That in April nights is heard.

And when weary lids would close,
  And thy head was drooping,
Then, like dew that steeps the rose,
  O'er thy languor stooping,
    I would, till I woke a sigh,
    Kiss thy sweet lips silently.

I would give thee all I own,
  All thou hast would borrow,
I from thee would keep alone
  Fear and doubt and sorrow.
    All of tender that is mine
    Should most tenderly be thine.

Moonlight! into other skies,
  I beseech thee wander.
Cruel thus to mock mine eyes,
  Idle, thus to squander
    Love's own light on this dark spot; —
    For my lady cometh not!

THOMAS LOVELL BEDDOES.

1803–1849

DREAM-PEDLARY.

I.

IF there were dreams to sell,
  What would you buy?
Some cost a passing bell;
  Some a light sigh,
That shakes from Life's fresh crown
Only a rose-leaf down.
If there were dreams to sell,
Merry and sad to tell,
And the crier rung the bell,
  What would you buy?

II.

A cottage lone and still,
  With bowers nigh,
Shadowy, my woes to still,
  Until I die.
Such pearl from Life's fresh crown
Fain would I shake me down.
Were dreams to have at will,
This would best heal my ill,
  This would I buy.

III.

But there were dreams to sell
  Ill didst thou buy;
Life is a dream, they tell,
  Waking, to die.
Dreaming a dream to prize,
Is wishing ghosts to rise;
  And, if I had the spell
  To call the buried well,
    Which one would I?

IV.

If there are ghosts to raise,
  What shall I call,
Out of hell's murky haze,
  Heaven's blue pall?
Raise my loved long-lost boy
To lead me to his joy.—
  There are no ghosts to raise;
  Out of death lead no ways;
    Vain is the call.

V.

Know'st thou not ghosts to sue
  No love thou hast.
Else lie, as I will do,
  And breathe thy last.
So out of Life's fresh crown
Fall like a rose-leaf down.
  Thus are the ghosts to woo;
  Thus are all dreams made true,
    Ever to last!

SONG FROM THE SHIP.

FROM "DEATH'S JEST-BOOK."

TO sea, to sea! the calm is o'er;
The wanton water leaps in sport,
And rattles down the pebbly shore;
The dolphin wheels, the sea-cows snort,
And unseen Mermaids' pearly song
Comes bubbling up, the weeds among.
Fling broad the sail, dip deep the oar:
To sea, to sea! the calm is o'er.

To sea, to sea! Our wide-winged bark
Shall billowy cleave its sunny way,
And with its shadow, fleet and dark,
Break the caved Tritons' azure day,
Like mighty eagle soaring light
O'er antelopes on Alpine height.
The anchor heaves, the ship swings free,
The sails swell full. To sea, to sea!

SONG.

MY goblet's golden lips are dry,
And, as the rose doth pine
For dew, so doth for wine
My goblet's cup;
Rain, O! rain, or it will die;
Rain, fill it up!

Arise, and get thee wings to-night,
Ætna! and let run o'er
Thy wines, a hill no more,
But darkly frown
A cloud, where eagles dare not soar,
Dropping rain down.

SONG.

FROM "THE SECOND BROTHER."

STREW not earth with empty stars,
Strew it not with roses,
Nor feathers from the crest of Mars,
Nor summer's idle posies.
'T is not the primrose-sandalled moon,
Nor cold and silent morn,
Nor he that climbs the dusty noon,
Nor mower war with scythe that drops,
Stuck with helmed and turbaned tops
Of enemies new shorn.
Ye cups, ye lyres, ye trumpets know,
Pour your music, let it flow,
'T is Bacchus' son who walks below.

SONG, BY TWO VOICES.

FROM "THE BRIDES' TRAGEDY."

FIRST VOICE.

WHO is the baby, that doth lie
Beneath the silken canopy
Of thy blue eye?

SECOND.

It is young Sorrow, laid asleep
In the crystal deep.

BOTH.

Let us sing his lullaby,
Heigho! a sob and a sigh.

FIRST VOICE.

What sound is that, so soft, so clear,
Harmonious as a bubbled tear
Bursting, we hear?

SECOND.

It is young Sorrow, slumber breaking,
Suddenly awaking.

BOTH.

Let us sing his lullaby,
Heigho! a sob and a sigh.

SONG.

FROM "TORRISMOND."

HOW many times do I love thee, dear?
Tell me how many thoughts there be
In the atmosphere
Of a new-fall'n year,
Whose white and sable hours appear
The latest flake of Eternity: —
So many times do I love thee, dear.

How many times do I love again?
Tell me how many beads there are
In a silver chain
Of evening rain,
Unravelled from the tumbling main,
And threading the eye of a yellow star: —
So many times do I love again.

WILLIAM COX BENNETT.

1820

CRADLE SONG.

SLEEP! the bird is in its nest;
Sleep! the bee is hushed in rest;
Sleep! rocked on thy mother's breast!
Lullaby!
To thy mother's fond heart pressed,
Lullaby!

Sleep! the waning daylight dies;
Sleep! the stars dream in the skies;
Daisies long have closed their eyes;
Lullaby!
Calm, how calm on all things lies!
Lullaby!

Sleep then, sleep! my heart's delight!
Sleep! and through the darksome night
Round thy bed God's angels bright
Lullaby!
Guard thee till I come with light!
Lullaby!

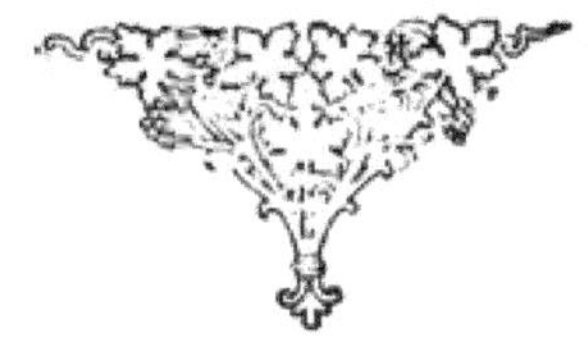

MY ROSES BLOSSOM THE WHOLE YEAR ROUND.

MY roses blossom the whole year round;
For, O they grow on enchanted ground;
Divine is the earth
Where they spring to birth;
On dimpling cheeks with love and mirth,
They 're found
They 're ever found.

My lilies no change of seasons heed;
Nor shelter from storms or frosts they need;
For, O they grow
On a neck of snow,
Nor all the wintry blasts that blow
They heed,
They ever heed.

CRADLE SONG.

LULLABY! O lullaby!
Baby, hush that little cry!
Light is dying,
Bats are flying,
Bees to-day with work have done;
So, till comes the morrow's sun,
Let sleep kiss those bright eyes dry!
Lullaby! O lullaby!

Lullaby! O lullaby!
Hushed are all things far and nigh;
Flowers are closing,
Birds reposing,
All sweet things with life have done;
Sweet, till dawns the morning sun,
Sleep then kiss those blue eyes dry!
Lullaby! O lullaby!

F. W. BOURDILLON.

1852.

LOVE'S MEINIE.

THERE is no summer ere the swallows come,
Nor Love appears,
Till Hope, Love's light-winged herald, lifts the gloom
Of years.

There is no summer left when swallows fly,
And Love at last,
When hopes which filled its heaven droop and die,
Is past.

THE NIGHT HAS A THOUSAND EYES.

THE night has a thousand eyes,
And the day but one;
Yet the light of the bright world dies
With the dying sun.

The mind has a thousand eyes,
And the heart but one;
Yet the light of a whole life dies
When love is done.

A LOST VOICE.

A THOUSAND voices fill my ears
  All day until the light grows pale;
But silence falls when night-time nears,
  And where art thou, sweet nightingale?

Was that thine echo, faint and far?
  Nay, all is hushed as heaven above;
In earth no voice, in heaven no star,
  And in my heart no dream of love.

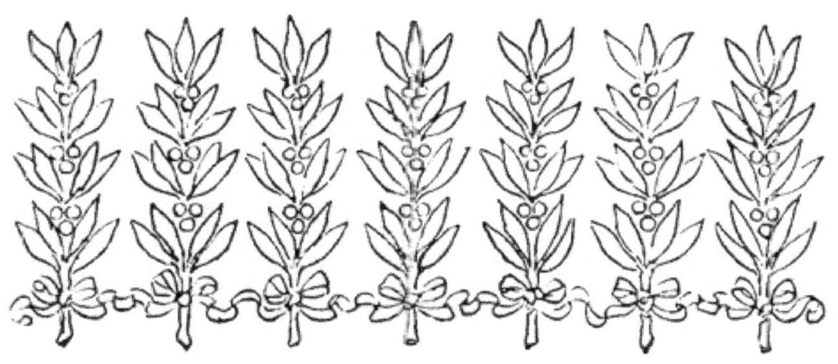

ROBERT BUCHANAN.

SERENADE.

SLEEP sweet, belovëd one, sleep sweet!
  Without here night is growing,
The dead leaf falls, the dark boughs meet,
  And a chill wind is blowing.
Strange shapes are stirring in the night,
  To the deep breezes wailing,
And slow, with wistful gleams of light,
  The storm-tost moon is sailing.

Sleep sweet, belovëd one, sleep sweet!
  Fold thy white hands, my blossom!
Thy warm limbs in thy lily sheet,
  Thy hands upon thy bosom.

Though evil thoughts may walk the dark,
  Not one shall near thy chamber;
But shapes divine shall pause to mark,
  Singing to lutes of amber.

Sleep sweet, belovëd one, sleep sweet!
  Though, on thy bosom creeping,
Strange hands are laid, to feel the beat
  Of thy soft heart in sleeping.
The brother angels, Sleep and Death,
  Stop by thy couch and eye thee;
And Sleep stoops down to drink thy breath,
  While Death goes softly by thee!

SONG.

FROM "LOVE IN WINTER."

"O LOVE is like the roses,
And every rose shall fall,
For sure as summer closes
They perish one and all.
Then love, while leaves are on the tree,
And birds sing in the bowers:
When winter comes, too late 't will be
To pluck the happy flowers."

"O Love is like the roses,
Love comes, and Love must flee!
Before the summer closes
Love's rapture and Love's glee!"

MORTIMER COLLINS.

1827 1876

TO F. C.

20TH FEBRUARY 1875.

FAST falls the snow, O lady mine,
Sprinkling the lawn with crystals fine,
But by the gods we won't repine
While we 're together,
We 'll chat and rhyme and kiss and dine,
Defying weather.

So stir the fire and pour the wine,
And let those sea-green eyes divine
Pour their love-madness into mine:
I don't care whether
'T is snow or sun or rain or shine
If we 're together.

A GAME OF CHESS.

TERRACE and lawn are white with frost,
Whose fretwork flowers upon the panes—
A mocking dream of summer, lost
'Mid winter's icy chains.

White-hot, indoors, the great logs gleam,
Veiled by a flickering flame of blue:
I see my love as in a dream—
Her eyes are azure, too.

She puts her hair behind her ears
(Each little ear so like a shell),
Touches her ivory Queen, and fears
She is not playing well.

For me, I think of nothing less:
I think how those pure pearls become her—
And which is sweetest, winter chess
Or garden strolls in summer.

O linger, frost, upon the pane!
  O faint blue flame, still softly rise!
O, dear one, thus with me remain,
    That I may watch thine eyes!

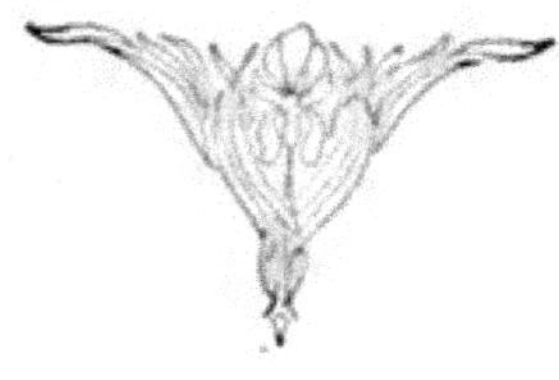

MULTUM IN PARVO.

A LITTLE shadow makes the sunrise sad,
A little trouble checks the race of joy,
A little agony may drive men mad,
A little madness may the soul destroy:
Such is the world's annoy.

Ay, and the rose is but a little flower
Which the red Queen of all the garden is:
And Love, which lasteth but a little hour,
A moment's rapture and a moment's kiss,
Is what no man would miss.

VIOLETS AT HOME.

I.

O HAPPY buds of violet!
I give thee to my sweet, and she
Puts them where something sweeter yet
Must always be.

II.

White violets find whiter rest:
For fairest flowers how fair a fate!
For me remain, O fragrant breast!
Inviolate.

MY THRUSH.

ALL through the sultry hours of June,
From morning blithe to golden noon,
And till the star of evening climbs
The gray-blue East, a world too soon,
There sings a Thrush amid the limes.

God's poet, hid in foliage green,
Sings endless songs, himself unseen;
Right seldom come his silent times.
Linger, ye summer hours serene!
Sing on, dear Thrush, amid the limes.

. . . .

May I not dream God sends thee there,
Thou mellow angel of the air,
Even to rebuke my earthlier rhymes
With music's soul, all praise and prayer?
Is that thy lesson in the limes?

Closer to God art thou than I:
His minstrel thou, whose brown wings fly
  Through silent æther's sunnier climes.
Ah, never may thy music die!
  Sing on, dear Thrush, amid the limes!

DINAH MARIA MULOCK CRAIK.

1826-1887.

TOO LATE.

"Douglas, Douglas, tendir and treu."

COULD ye come back to me, Douglas, Douglas,
In the old likeness that I knew,
I would be so faithful, so loving, Douglas,
Douglas, Douglas, tender and true.

Never a scornful word should grieve ye,
I'd smile on ye sweet as the angels do;—
Sweet as your smile on me shone ever,
Douglas, Douglas, tender and true.

O to call back the days that are not!
My eyes were blinded, your words were few:
Do you know the truth now up in heaven,
Douglas, Douglas, tender and true?

I never was worthy of you, Douglas;
  Not half worthy the like of you:
Now all men beside seem to me like shadows —
  I love *you*, Douglas, tender and true.

Stretch out your hand to me, Douglas, Douglas,
  Drop forgiveness from heaven like dew;
As I lay my heart on your dead heart, Douglas,
  Douglas, Douglas, tender and true.

A SILLY SONG.

"O HEART, my heart!" she said, and heard
His mate the blackbird calling,
While through the sheen of the garden green
May rain was softly falling,—
Aye softly, softly falling.

The buttercups across the field
Made sunshine rifts of splendour:
The round snow-bud of the thorn in the wood
Peeped through its leafage tender,
As the rain came softly falling.

"O heart, my heart!" she said and smiled,
"There 's not a tree of the valley,
Or a leaf I wis which the rain's soft kiss
Freshens in yonder alley,
Where the drops keep ever falling,—

"There 's not a foolish flower i' the grass,
Or bird through the woodland calling,
So glad again of the coming rain
As I of these tears now falling, —
These happy tears down falling."

GEORGE DARLEY.

1795-1846.

MAY DAY.

FROM "SYLVIA": *Act III. Scene ii.*

O MAY, thou art a merry time,
  Sing hi! the hawthorn pink and pale!
When hedge-pipes they begin to chime,
  And summer-flowers to sow the dale.

When lasses and their lovers meet
  Beneath the early village-thorn,
And to the sound of tabor sweet
  Bid welcome to the Maying-morn!

O May, thou art a merry time,
  Sing hi! the hawthorn pink and pale!
When hedge-pipes they begin to chime,
  And summer-flowers to sow the dale.

When grey-beards and their gossips come
  With crutch in hand our sports to see,
And both go tottering, tattling home,
  Topful of wine as well as glee!

O May, thou art a merry time,
  Sing hi! the hawthorn pink and pale!
When hedge-pipes they begin to chime,
  And summer-flowers to sow the dale.

But Youth was aye the time for bliss,
  So taste it, Shepherds! while ye may:
For who can tell that joy like this
  Will come another holiday?

O May, thou art a merry time,
  Sing hi! the hawthorn pink and pale!
When hedge-pipes they begin to chime,
  And summer-flowers to sow the dale.

I'VE BEEN ROAMING.

FROM "LILIAN OF THE VALE."

I 'VE been roaming! I 've been roaming!
  Where the meadow dew is sweet,
And like a queen I 'm coming
  With its pearls upon my feet.

I 've been roaming! I 've been roaming!
  O'er red rose and lily fair,
And like a sylph I 'm coming
  With their blossoms in my hair.

I 've been roaming! I 've been roaming!
  Where the honeysuckle creeps,
And like a bee I 'm coming
  With its kisses on my lips.

I 've been roaming! I 've been roaming!
  Over hill and over plain,
And like a bird I 'm coming
  To my bower back again!

SYLVIA'S SONG.

THE streams that wind amid the hills
And lost in pleasure slowly roam,
While their deep joy the valley fills,—
Even these will leave their mountain home;
So may it, Love! with others be,
But I will never wend from thee.

The leaf forsakes the parent spray,
The blossom quits the stem as fast;
The rose-enamour'd bird will stray
And leave his eglantine at last:
So may it, Love! with others be,
But I will never wend from thee.

SERENADE.

FROM "SYLVIA": *Act IV. Scene I.*

ROMANZO SINGS:

AWAKE thee, my Lady-love!
Wake thee, and rise!
The sun through the bower peeps
Into thine eyes!

Behold how the early lark
Springs from the corn!
Hark, hark how the flower-bird
Winds her wee horn!

The swallow's glad shriek is heard
All through the air!
The stock-dove is murmuring
Loud as she dare!

Apollo's winged bugleman
Cannot contain,
But peals his loud trumpet-call
Once and again!

Then wake thee, my Lady-love,
  Bird of my bower!
The sweetest and sleepiest
  Bird at this hour!

LORD DE TABLEY.

1835.

A WINTER SKETCH.

WHEN the snow begins to feather,
And the woods begin to roar
Clashing angry beughs together,
As the breakers grind the shore
Nature then a bankrupt goes,
Full of wreck and full of woes.

When the swan for warmer forelands
Leaves the sea-firth's icebound edge,
When the gray geese from the morelands
Cleave the clouds in noisy wedge,
Woodlands stand in frozen chains,
Hung with ropes of solid rains.

Shepherds creep to byre and haven,
  Sheep in drifts are nipped and numb;
Some belated rook or raven
  Rocks upon a sign-post dumb;
Mere-waves, solid as a clod,
Roar with skaters, thunder-shod.

All the roofs and chimneys rumble;
  Roads are ridged with slush and sleet;
Down the orchard apples tumble;
  Ploughboys stamp their frosty feet;
Millers, jolted down the lanes,
Hardly feel for cold their reins.

Snipes are calling from the trenches,
  Frozen half and half at flow;
In the porches servant wenches
  Work with shovels at the snow;
Rusty blackbirds, weak of wing,
Clean forget they once could sing.

Dogs and boys fetch down the cattle,
  Deep in mire and powdered pale;

Spinning-wheels commence to rattle;
  Landlords spice the smoking ale.
Hail, white winter, lady fine,
In a cup of elder wine!

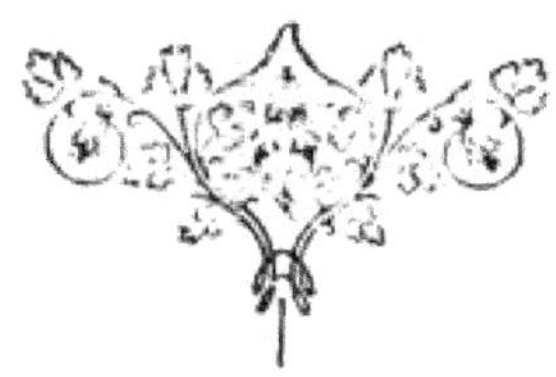

THE SECOND MADRIGAL.

WOO thy lass while May is here;
  Winter vows are colder.
Have thy kiss when lips are near;
  To-morrow you are older.

Think, if clear the throstle sing,
  A month his note will thicken;
A throat of gold in a golden spring
  At the edge of the snow will sicken.

Take thy cup and take thy girl,
  While they come for asking;
In thy heydey melt the pearl
  At the love-ray basking.

Ale is good for careless bards,
  Wine for wayworn sinners.
They who hold the strongest cards
  Rise from life as winners.

AUBREY DE VERE.

1788-1846.

SONG.

I.

SOFTLY, O midnight Hours!
Move softly o'er the bowers
Where lies in happy sleep a girl so fair!
For ye have power, men say,
Our hearts in sleep to sway,
And cage cold fancies in a moonlight snare.
Round ivory neck and arm
Enclasp a separate charm:
Hang o'er her poised; but breathe nor sigh nor prayer:
Silently ye may smile,
But hold your breath the while,
And let the wind sweep back your cloudy hair!

II.

Bend down your glittering urns
Ere yet the dawn returns,
And star with dew the lawn her feet shall tread;
Upon the air rain balm;
Bid all the woods be calm;
Ambrosial dreams with healthful slumbers wed.
That so the Maiden may
With smiles your care repay
When from her couch she lifts her golden head;
Waking with earliest birds,
Ere yet the misty herds
Leave warm 'mid the grey grass their dusky bed.

SONG.

SEEK not the tree of silkiest bark
    And balmiest bud,
To carve her name — while yet 't is dark —
    Upon the wood!
The world is full of noble tasks
    And wreaths hard-won:
Each work demands strong hearts, strong hands,
    Till day is done.

Sing not that violet-veinèd skin,
    That cheek's pale roses;
The lily of that form wherein
    Her soul reposes!
Forth to the fight, true man, true knight!
    The clash of arms
Shall more prevail than whispered tale
    To win her charms.

Aubrey de Vere.

The warrior for the True, the Right,
  Fights in Love's name:
The love that lures thee from that fight
  Lures thee to shame.
That love which lifts the heart, yet leaves
  The spirit free,—
That love, or none, is fit for one,
  Man-shaped like thee.

SONG.

I.

WHEN I was young, I said to Sorrow,
"Come, and I will play with thee:"—
He is near me now all day;
And at night returns to say,
"I will come again to-morrow,
I will come and stay with thee."

II.

Through the woods we walk together;
His soft footsteps rustle nigh me;
To shield an unregarded head,
He hath built a winter shed;
And all night in rainy weather,
I hear his gentle breathings by me.

CHARLES DICKENS.

1812-1870

THE IVY GREEN.

OH, a dainty plant is the Ivy green,
That creepeth o'er ruins old!
Of right choice food are his meals I ween,
In his cell so lone and cold.
The wall must be crumbled, the stone decayed,
To pleasure his dainty whim:
And the mouldering dust that years have made
Is a merry meal for him.
Creeping where no life is seen,
A rare old plant is the Ivy green.

Fast he stealeth on, though he wears no wings,
And a staunch old heart has he.
How closely he twineth, how tight he clings,
To his friend, the huge Oak tree!

And slily he traileth along the ground,
And his leaves he gently waves,
As he joyously hugs and crawleth round
The rich mould of dead men's graves.
Creeping where grim death has been,
A rare old plant is the Ivy green.

Whole ages have fled, and their works decayed,
And nations have scattered been;
But the stout old Ivy shall never fade
From its hale and hearty green.
The brave old plant in its lonely days
Shall fatten upon the past:
For the stateliest building man can raise
Is the Ivy's food at last.
Creeping on, where time has been,
A rare old plant is the Ivy green.

AUSTIN DOBSON.

1840.

THE LADIES OF ST. JAMES'S.

A PROPER NEW BALLAD OF THE COUNTRY AND THE TOWN.

THE ladies of St. James's
Go swinging to the play;
Their footmen run before them,
With a "Stand by! Clear the way!"
But Phyllida, my Phyllida!
She takes her buckled shoon,
When we go out a-courting
Beneath the harvest moon.

The ladies of St. James's
Wear satin on their backs;
They sit all night at *Ombre*,
With candles all of wax:

But Phyllida, my Phyllida!
  She dons her russet gown,
And runs to gather May dew
  Before the world is down.

The ladies of St. James's
  They are so fine and fair,
You 'd think a box of essences
  Was broken in the air:
But Phyllida, my Phyllida!
  The breath of heath and furze,
When breezes blow at morning,
  Is scarce so fresh as hers.

The ladies of St. James's
  They 're painted to the eyes;
Their white it stays forever,
  Their red it never dies:
But Phyllida, my Phyllida!
  Her color comes and goes;
It trembles to a lily,
  It wavers to a rose.

The ladies of St. James's,
  With "Mercy!" and with "Lud!"
They season all their speeches
  (They come of noble blood):
But Phyllida, my Phyllida!
  Her shy and simple words
Are sweet as, after rain-drops,
  The music of the birds.

The ladies of St. James's,
  They have their fits and freaks;
They smile on you — for seconds,
  They frown on you — for weeks:
But Phyllida, my Phyllida!
  Come either storm or shine,
From Shrovetide unto Shrovetide
  Is always true — and mine.

My Phyllida, my Phyllida!
  I care not though they heap
The hearts of all St. James's,
  And give me all to keep;

I care not whose the beauties
  Of all the world may be,
For Phyllida — for Phyllida
  Is all the world to me!

THE MILKMAID.

A NEW SONG TO AN OLD TUNE.

ACROSS the grass I see her pass;
  She comes with tripping pace, —
A maid I know, — and March winds blow
  Her hair across her face; —
    With a hey, Dolly! ho, Dolly!
      Dolly shall be mine,
    Before the spray is white with May,
      Or blooms the eglantine.

The March winds blow. I watch her go:
  Her eye is brown and clear;
Her cheek is brown and soft as down
  (To those who see it near!) —
    With a hey, Dolly! ho, Dolly!
      Dolly shall be mine,
    Before the spray is white with May,
      Or blooms the eglantine.

What has she not that they have got,—
  The dames that walk in silk!
If she undo her 'kerchief blue,
  Her neck is white as milk.
    With a hey, Dolly! ho, Dolly!
      Dolly shall be mine,
    Before the spray is white with May,
      Or blooms the eglantine.

Let those who will be proud and chill!
  For me, from June to June,
My Dolly's words are sweet as curds,—
  Her laugh is like a tune;—
    With a hey, Dolly! ho, Dolly!
      Dolly shall be mine,
    Before the spray is white with May,
      Or blooms the eglantine.

Break, break to hear, O crocus-spear!
  O tall Lent-lilies, flame!
There'll be a bride at Easter-tide,
  And Dolly is her name.

"A maid I knew, ... and March winds blow
Her hair across her face"

With a hey, Dolly! ho, Dolly!
  Dolly shall be mine,
Before the spray is white with May,
  Or blooms the eglantine.

ALFRED DOMETT.

1811-1887.

A GLEE FOR WINTER.

HENCE, rude Winter! crabbed old fellow,
Never merry, never mellow!
Well-a-day! in rain and snow
What will keep one's heart aglow?
Groups of kinsmen, old and young,
Oldest they old friends among!
Groups of friends, so old and true,
That they seem our kinsmen too!
These all merry all together,
Charm away chill Winter weather!

What will kill this dull old fellow?
Ale that 's bright, and wine that 's mellow!
Dear old songs for ever new;
Some true love, and laughter too;

Pleasant wit, and harmless fun,
And a dance when day is done!
Music — friends so true and tried —
Whispered love by warm fireside —
Mirth at all times all together —
Make sweet May of Winter weather!

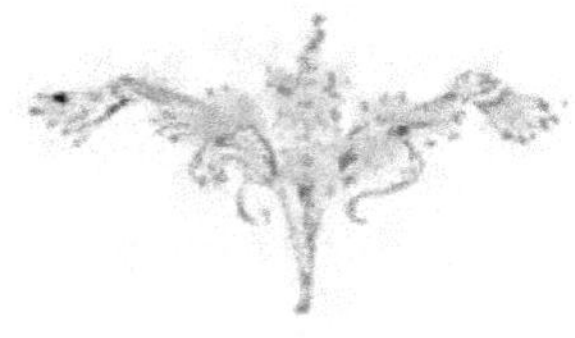

A KISS.

SAPPHO TO PHAON.

I.

SWEET mouth! O let me take
One draught from that delicious cup!
The hot Sahara-thirst to slake
That burns me up!

II.

Sweet breath!—all flowers that are,
Within that darling frame must bloom;
My heart revives so at the rare
Divine perfume!

III.

—Nay, 't is a dear deceit,
A drunkard's cup that mouth of thine;
Sure poison-flowers are breathing, sweet,
That fragrance fine!

IV.

I drank—the drink betrayed me
Into a madder, fiercer fever;
The scent of those love-blossoms made me
More faint than ever!

V.

Yet though quick death it were
That rich heart-vintage I must drain,
And quaff that hidden garden's air,
Again—again!

LADY DUFFERIN.

1807-1867.

*SONG.**

APRIL 30, 1833.

I.

WHEN another's voice thou hearest,
With a sad and gentle tone,
Let its sound but waken, dearest,
Memory of *my* love alone!
When in stranger lands thou meetest
Warm, true hearts, which welcome thee,
Let each friendly look thou greetest
Seem a message, Love, from *me!*

* These lines were written to the author's husband, then at sea, in 1833, and set to music by herself.

II.

When night's quiet sky is o'er thee,
  When the pale stars dimly burn,
Dream that *one* is watching for thee,
  Who but lives for thy return!
Wheresoe'er thy steps are roving,
  Night or day, by land or sea,
Think of her, whose life of loving
  Is but one long thought of thee!

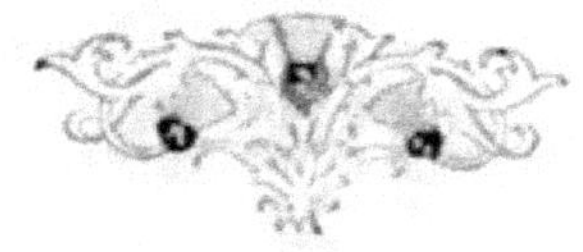

LAMENT OF THE IRISH EMIGRANT.

I'M sitting on the stile, Mary,
  Where we sat, side by side,
That bright May morning long ago
  When first you were my bride.
The corn was springing fresh and green,
  The lark sang loud and high,
The red was on your lip, Mary,
  The love-light in your eye.

The place is little changed, Mary,
  The day is bright as then,
The lark's loud song is in my ear,
  The corn is green again;
But I miss the soft clasp of your hand,
  Your breath warm on my cheek,
And I still keep list'ning for the words
  You never more may speak.

'T is but a step down yonder lane,
  The little Church stands near —
The Church where we were wed, Mary, —
  I see the spire from here;
But the graveyard lies between, Mary, —
  My step might break your rest, —
Where you, my darling, lie asleep
  With your baby on your breast.

I 'm very lonely now, Mary, —
  The poor make no new friends; —
But, oh! they love the better still
  The few our Father sends.
And you were all I had, Mary,
  My blessing and my pride;
There 's nothing left to care for now
  Since my poor Mary died.

Yours was the good brave heart, Mary,
  That still kept hoping on,
When trust in God had left my soul,
  And half my strength was gone.

There was comfort ever on your lip,
  And the kind look on your brow.
I bless you, Mary, for that same,
  Though you can't hear me now.

I thank you for the patient smile
  When your heart was fit to break;
When the hunger pain was gnawing there
  You hid it for my sake.
I bless you for the pleasant word
  When your heart was sad and sore.
Oh! I'm thankful you are gone, Mary,
  Where grief can't reach you more!

I'm bidding you a long farewell,
  My Mary — kind and true!
But I'll not forget you, darling,
  In the land I'm going to.
They say there's bread and work for all,
  And the sun shines always there;
But I'll not forget old Ireland,
  Were it fifty times as fair.

And when amid those grand old woods
  I sit and shut my eyes,
My heart will travel back again
  To where my Mary lies;
I 'll think I see the little stile
  Where we sat, side by side, —
And the springing corn and bright May morn,
  When first you were my bride.

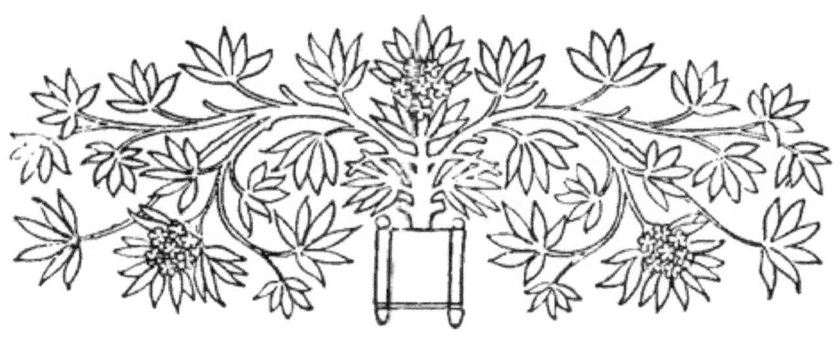

MICHAEL FIELD.

WINDS TO-DAY ARE LARGE AND FREE.

WINDS to-day are large and free,
Winds to-day are westerly;
From the land they seem to blow
Whence the sap begins to flow
And the dimpled light to spread,
From the country of the dead.

Ah, it is a wild, sweet land
Where the coming May is planned,
Where such influences throb
As our frosts can never rob
Of their triumph, when they bound
Through the tree and from the ground.

Great within me is my soul,
Great to journey to its goal,
To the country of the dead;
For the cornel-tips are red,
And a passion rich in strife
Drives me toward the home of life.

Oh, to keep the spring with them
Who have flushed the cornel-stem,
Who imagine at its source
All the year's delicious course,
Then express by wind and light
Something of their rapture's height!

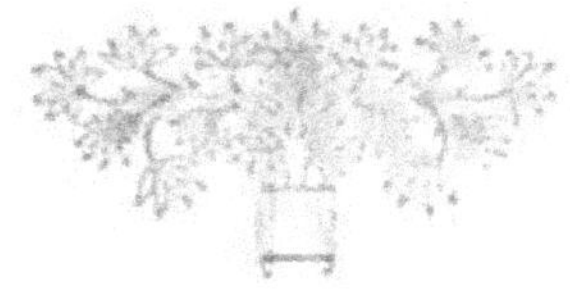

LET US WREATHE THE MIGHTY CUP.

LET us wreathe the mighty cup,
Then with song we 'll lift it up,
And, before we drain the glow
Of the juice that foams below
Flowers and cool leaves round the brim,
Let us swell the praise of him
Who is tyrant of the heart,
Cupid with his flaming dart!

Pride before his face is bowed,
Strength and heedless beauty cowed;
Underneath his fatal wings
Bend discrowned the heads of kings;
Maidens blanch beneath his eye
And its laughing mastery;
Through each land his arrows sound,
By his fetters all are bound.

WHERE WINDS ABOUND.

WHERE winds abound,
And fields are hilly,
Shy daffadilly
Looks down on the ground.

Rose cones of larch
Are just beginning;
Though oaks are spinning
No oak-leaves in March.

Spring 's at the core,
The boughs are sappy:
Good to be happy
So long, long before!

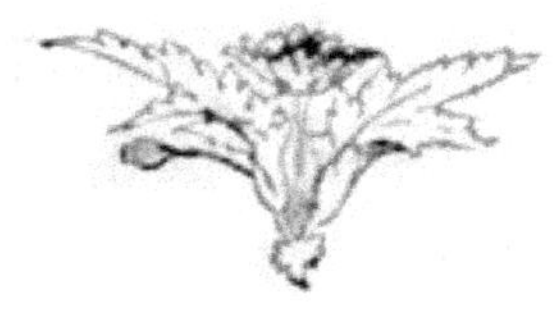

NORMAN GALE.

1862

A SONG.

FIRST the fine, faint, dreamy motion
  Of the tender blood
Circling in the veins of children—
  This is Life, the bud.

Next the fresh, advancing beauty
  Growing from the gloom,
Waking eyes and fuller bosom—
  This is Life, the bloom.

Then the pain that follows after,
  Grievous to be borne,
Pricking, steeped in subtle poison—
  This is Love, the thorn.

SONG.

WAIT but a little while —
  The bird will bring
A heart in tune for melodies
  Unto the spring,
Till he who 's in the cedar there
Is moved to trill a song so rare,
And pipe her fair.

Wait but a little while —
  The bud will break;
The inner rose will ope and glow
  For summer's sake;
Fond bees will lodge within her breast
Till she herself is plucked and prest
Where I would rest.

Wait but a little while —
  The maid will grow

Gracious with lips and hands to thee,
  With breast of snow.
To-day Love 's mute, but time hath sown
A soul in her to match thine own,
Though yet ungrown.

EDMUND GOSSE.

1849.

SONG FOR THE LUTE.

I BRING a garland for your head
  Of blossoms fresh and fair;
My own hands wound their white and red
  To ring about your hair:
Here is a lily, here a rose,
A warm narcissus that scarce blows,
And fairer blossoms no man knows.

So crowned and chapleted with flowers,
  I pray you be not proud;
For after brief and summer hours
  Comes autumn with a shroud;—
Though fragrant as a flower you lie,
You and your garland, bye and bye,
Will fade and wither up and die.

THOMAS HOOD.

1798-1845.

BALLAD.

I.

IT was not in the winter
  Our loving lot was cast;
It was the time of roses,—
We plucked them as we passed;

II.

That churlish season never frowned
On early lovers yet:—
Oh, no—the world was newly crowned
With flowers when first we met!

III.

'T was twilight, and I bade you go,
But still you held me fast;
It was the time of roses,—
We plucked them as we passed.—

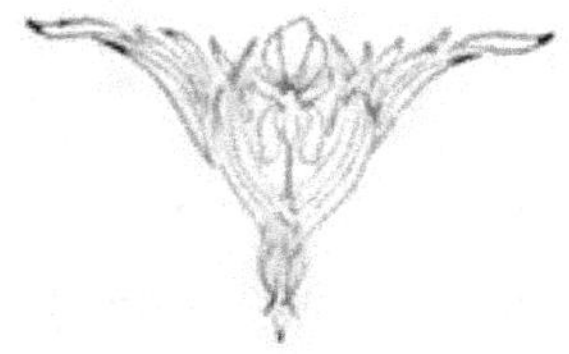

SONG.

O LADY, leave thy silken thread
And flowery tapestrie:
There 's living roses on the bush,
And blossoms on the tree;
Stoop where thou wilt, thy careless hand
Some random bud will meet;
Thou canst not tread, but thou wilt find
The daisy at thy feet.

'T is like the birthday of the world,
When earth was born in bloom;
The light is made of many dyes,
The air is all perfume;
There 's crimson buds, and white and blue—
The very rainbow showers
Have turned to blossoms where they fell,
And sown the earth with flowers.

There 's fairy tulips in the east,
  The garden of the sun;
The very streams reflect the hues,
  And blossom as they run:
While Morn opes like a crimson rose,
  Still wet with pearly showers;
Then, Lady, leave the silken thread
  Thou twinest into flowers!

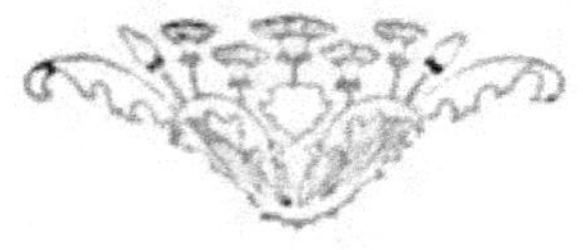

I REMEMBER, I REMEMBER.

I REMEMBER, I remember,
The house where I was born,
The little window where the sun
Came peeping in at morn;
He never came a wink too soon,
Nor brought too long a day,
But now, I often wish the night
Had borne my breath away!

I remember, I remember,
The roses, red and white,
The vi'lets, and the lily-cups,
Those flowers made of light!
The lilacs where the robin built,
And where my brother set
The laburnum on his birthday,—
The tree is living yet!

I remember, I remember
Where I was used to swing,
And thought the air must rush as fresh
To swallows on the wing;
My spirit flew in feathers then,
That is so heavy now,
And summer pools could hardly cool
The fever on my brow!

I remember, I remember
The fir trees dark and high;
I used to think their slender tops
Were close against the sky:
It was a childish ignorance,
But now 't is little joy
To know I 'm farther off from heav'n
Than when I was a boy.

BALLAD.

SHE 'S up and gone, the graceless Girl!
  And robbed my failing years;
My blood before was thin and cold
  But now 't is turned to tears;—
My shadow falls upon my grave,
  So near the brink I stand,
She might have stayed a little yet,
  And led me by the hand!

Ay, call her on the barren moor,
  And call her on the hill,
'T is nothing but the heron's cry,
  And plover's answer shrill;
My child is flown on wilder wings,
  Than they have ever spread,
And I may even walk a waste
  That widened when she fled.

Full many a thankless child has been,
  But never one like mine;
Her meat was served on plates of gold,
  Her drink was rosy wine;
But now she'll share the robin's food,
  And sup the common rill,
Before her feet will turn again
  To meet her father's will!

SONG.

I.

THE stars are with the voyager
  Wherever he may sail;
The moon is constant to her time;
  The sun will never fail;
But follow, follow round the world,
  The green earth and the sea;
So love is with the lover's heart,
  Wherever he may be.

II.

Wherever he may be, the stars
  Must daily lose their light;
The moon will veil her in the shade;
  The sun will set at night.
The sun may set, but constant love
  Will shine when he 's away;
So that dull night is never night,
  And day is brighter day.

RICHARD MONCKTON MILNES (LORD HOUGHTON).

1809–1885.

THE BROOKSIDE.

I WANDERED by the brook-side,
  I wandered by the mill, —
I could not hear the brook flow,
  The noisy wheel was still;
There was no burr of grasshopper,
  No chirp of any bird,
But the beating of my own heart
  Was all the sound I heard.

I sat beside the elm-tree,
  I watched the long, long, shade,
And as it grew still longer,
  I did not feel afraid;

For I listened for a footfall,
  I listened for a word,—
But the beating of my own heart
  Was all the sound I heard.

He came not,—no, he came not,—
  The night came on alone,—
The little stars sat one by one,
  Each on his golden throne;
The evening air passed by my cheek,
  The leaves above were stirred,—
But the beating of my own heart
  Was all the sound I heard.

Fast silent tears were flowing,
  When something stood behind,—
A hand was on my shoulder,
  I knew its touch was kind:
It drew me nearer—nearer,—
  We did not speak one word,
For the beating of our own hearts
  Was all the sound we heard.

"I wandered by the brook side"

THE VENETIAN SERENADE.

WHEN along the light ripple the far serenade
Has accosted the ear of each passionate maid,
She may open the window that looks on the stream, —
She may smile on her pillow and blend it in dream;
Half in words, half in music, it pierces the gloom,
"I am coming — Stali * — but you know not for whom!
Stali — not for whom!"

Now the tones become clearer, — you hear more and more
How the water divided returns on the oar, —
Does the prow of the Gondola strike on the stair?
Do the voices and instruments pause and prepare?
Oh! they faint on the ear as the lamp on the view,
"I am passing — Premi — but I stay not for you!
Premi — not for you!"

Then return to your couch, you who stifle a tear,
Then awake not, fair sleeper — believe he is here;

* The words here used are the calls of the gondoliers, indicating the direction they are rowing. "Sciàr" is to stop the boat.

For the young and the loving no sorrow endures,
If to-day be another's, — to-morrow is yours;
May, the next time you listen, your fancy be true,
"I am coming — Sciàr — and for you and to you!
Sciàr — and to you!"

FROM LOVE AND NATURE.

THE Sun came through the frosty mist
Most like a dead-white moon;
Thy soothing tones I seemed to list,
As voices in a swoon.

Still as an island stood our ship,
The waters gave no sound,
But when I touched thy quivering lip
I felt the world go round.

We seemed the only sentient things
Upon that silent sea:
Our hearts the only living springs
Of all that yet could be!

JEAN INGELOW.

1830.

THE LONG WHITE SEAM

AS I came round the harbor buoy,
  The lights began to gleam,
No wave the land-locked water stirred,
  The crags were white as cream;
And I marked my love by candle-light
  Sewing her long white seam.
    It 's aye sewing ashore, my dear,
      Watch and steer at sea,
    It 's reef and furl, and haul the line,
      Set sail and think of thee.

I climbed to reach her cottage door;
  O sweetly my love sings!

Like a shaft of light her voice breaks forth,
My soul to meet it springs
As the shining water leaped of old,
When stirred by angel wings.
Aye longing to list anew,
Awake and in my dream,
But never a song she sang like this,
Sewing her long white seam.

Fair fall the lights, the harbor lights,
That brought me in to thee,
And peace drop down on that low roof
For the sight that I did see,
And the voice, my dear, that rang so clear
All for the love of me.
For O, for O, with brows bent low
By the candle's flickering gleam,
Her wedding gown it was she wrought,
Sewing the long white seam.

LOVE.

FROM "SONGS OF SEVEN."

I LEANED out of window, I smelt the white clover,
Dark, dark was the garden, I saw not the gate;
"Now, if there be footsteps, he comes, my one lover—
Hush, nightingale, hush! O, sweet nightingale, wait
Till I listen and hear
If a step draweth near,
For my love he is late!

"The skies in the darkness stoop nearer and nearer,
A cluster of stars hangs like fruit in the tree,
The fall of the water comes sweeter, comes clearer:
To what art thou listening, and what dost thou see?
Let the star-clusters grow,
Let the sweet waters flow,
And cross quickly to me.

"You night moths that hover where honey brims over
From sycamore blossoms, or settle or sleep;

You glowworms, shine out, and the pathway discover
  To him that comes darkling along the rough steep.
    Ah, my sailor, make haste,
    For the time runs to waste,
    And my love lieth deep —

"Too deep for swift telling; and yet, my one lover,
  I've conned thee an answer, it waits thee to-night."
By the sycamore passed he, and through the white clover,
  Then all the sweet speech I had fashioned took flight;
    But I'll love him more, more
    Than e'er wife loved before,
    Be the days dark or bright.

SWEET IS CHILDHOOD.

SWEET is childhood — childhood 's over,
Kiss and part.
Sweet is youth; but youth 's a rover —
So 's my heart.
Sweet is rest; but by all showing
Toil is nigh.
We must go. Alas! the going,
Say "good-bye."

CHARLES KINGSLEY.

1819-1875

AIRLY BEACON.

AIRLY Beacon, Airly Beacon;
  Oh the pleasant sight to see
Shires and towns from Airly Beacon,
  While my love climbed up to me!

Airly Beacon, Airly Beacon;
  Oh the happy hours we lay
Deep in fern on Airly Beacon,
  Courting through the summer's day!

Airly Beacon, Airly Beacon;
  Oh the weary haunt for me,
All alone on Airly Beacon,
  With his baby on my knee!

THE SANDS OF DEE.

"OH, Mary, go and call the cattle home,
And call the cattle home,
And call the cattle home
Across the sands of Dee;"
The western wind was wild and dark with foam,
And all alone went she.

The western tide crept up along the sand,
And o'er and o'er the sand,
And round and round the sand,
As far as eye could see.
The rolling mist came down and hid the land:
And never home came she.

"Oh! is it weed, or fish, or floating hair —
A tress of golden hair,
A drownèd maiden's hair
Above the nets at sea?"
Was never salmon yet that shone so fair
Among the stakes on Dee.

They rowed her in across the rolling foam,
    The cruel crawling foam,
    The cruel hungry foam,
To her grave beside the sea:
But still the boatmen hear her call the cattle home
Across the sands of Dee.

THREE FISHERS WENT SAILING.

THREE fishers went sailing away to the West,
Away to the West as the sun went down;
Each thought on the woman who loved him the best,
And the children stood watching them out of the town;
For men must work, and women must weep,
And there 's little to earn, and many to keep,
Though the harbor bar be moaning.

Three wives sat up in the lighthouse tower,
And they trimmed the lamps as the sun went down;
They looked at the squall, and they looked at the shower,
And the night-rack came rolling up ragged and brown.
But men must work, and women must weep,
Though storms be sudden, and waters deep,
And the harbor bar be moaning.

" Three fishers went sailing away to the West"

Three corpses lay out on the shining sands
  In the morning gleam as the tide went down,
And the women are weeping and wringing their hands
  For those who will never come home to the town;
For men must work, and women must weep,
And the sooner it 's over, the sooner to sleep;
  And good-bye to the bar and its moaning.

A FAREWELL.

To C. E. G. — 1856.

MY fairest child, I have no song to give you;
No lark could pipe in skies so dull and gray;
Yet, if you will, one quiet hint I'll leave you,
For every day.

I'll tell you how to sing a clearer carol
Than lark who hails the dawn of breezy down;
To earn yourself a purer poet's laurel
Than Shakespeare's crown.

Be good, sweet maid, and let who can be clever;
Do lovely things, not dream them, all day long;
And so make Life, and Death, and that For Ever,
One grand sweet song.

WALTER SAVAGE LANDOR.

1775-1864.

ROSE AYLMER.

AH, what avails the sceptered race!
  Ah, what the form divine!
What every virtue, every grace!
  Rose Aylmer, all were thine.
Rose Aylmer, whom these wakeful eyes
  May weep, but never see,
A night of memories and of sighs
  I consecrate to thee.

RUBIES.

OFTEN I have heard it said
That her lips are ruby-red.
Little heed I what they say,
I have seen as red as they.
Ere she smiled on other men,
Real rubies were they then.

When she kissed me once in play,
Rubies were less bright than they,
And less bright were those which shone
In the palace of the Sun.
Will they be as bright again?
Not if kissed by other men.

THE FAULT IS NOT MINE.

THE fault is not mine if I love you too much,
I loved you too little too long,
Such ever your graces, your tenderness such,
And the music the heart gave the tongue.

A time is now coming when Love must be gone,
Tho' he never abandoned me yet.
Acknowledge our friendship, our passion disown,
Our follies (ah can you?) forget.

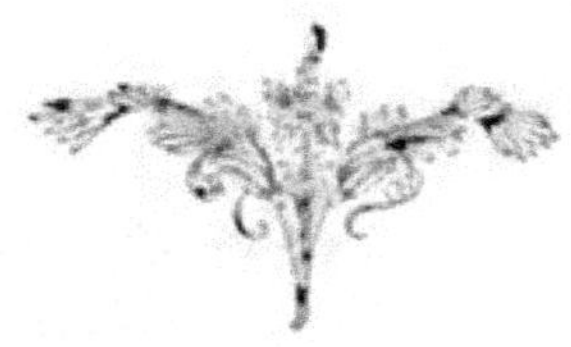

UNDER THE LINDENS.

UNDER the lindens lately sat
A couple, and no more, in chat;
I wondered what they would be at
Under the lindens.

I saw four eyes and four lips meet,
I heard the words, "*How sweet! how sweet!*"
Had then the Faeries given a treat
Under the lindens?

I pondered long and could not tell
What dainty pleased them both so well:
Bees! bees! was it your hydromel
Under the lindens?

SIXTEEN.

IN Clementina's artless mien
  Lucilla asks me what I see,—
And are the roses of sixteen
      Enough for me?

Lucilla asks, if that be all,
  Have I not culled as sweet before?
Ah yes, Lucilla! and their fall
      I still deplore.

I now behold another scene,
  Where Pleasure beams with heaven's own light,—
More pure, more constant, more serene,
      And not less bright:

Faith, on whose breast the Loves repose,
  Whose chain of flowers no force can sever,
And Modesty, who, when she goes,
      Is gone forever!

IANTHE.

THANK Heaven, Ianthe, once again
  Our hands and ardent lips shall meet,
And Pleasure, to assert his reign,
  Scatter ten thousand kisses sweet:
Then cease repeating while you mourn,
"I wonder when he will return."

Ah wherefore should you so admire
  The flowing words that fill my song,
Why call them artless, yet require
  "Some promise from that tuneful tongue?"
I doubt if heaven itself could part
A tuneful tongue and tender heart.

ONE LOVELY NAME.

ONE lovely name adorns my song,
And, dwelling in the heart,
For ever falters at the tongue,
And trembles to depart.

FORSAKEN.

MOTHER, I can not mind my wheel;
My fingers ache, my lips are dry;
Oh! if you felt the pain I feel!
But oh, who ever felt as I!
No longer could I doubt him true,
All other men may use deceit;
He always said my eyes were blue,
And often swore my lips were sweet.

FREDERICK LOCKER-LAMPSON.

1821–1895.

A GARDEN LYRIC.

The flow of life is yet a rill
  That laughs, and leaps, and glistens;
And still the woodland rings, and still
  The old Damœtas listens.

WE have loiter'd and laugh'd in the flowery croft,
  We have met under wintry skies;
Her voice is the dearest voice, and soft
  Is the light in her gentle eyes;
It is bliss in the silent woods, among
  Gay crowds, or in any place
To hear her voice, to gaze on her young
    Confiding face.

For ever may roses divinely blow,
  And wine-dark pansies charm
By the prim box path where I felt the glow
  Of her dimpled, trusting arm,
And the sweep of her silk as she turned and smiled
  A smile as pure as her pearls;
The breeze was in love with the darling Child,
    As it moved her curls.

She showed me her ferns and woodbine-sprays,
  Foxglove and jasmine stars,
A mist of blue in the beds, a blaze
  Of red in the celadon jars:
And velvety bees in convolvulus bells,
  And roses of bountiful June—
Oh, who would think their summer spells
    Could die so soon!

For a glad song came from the milking shed,
  On a wind of the summer south,
And the green was golden above her head,
  And a sunbeam kiss'd her mouth;

Sweet were the lips where that sunbeam dwelt;
  And the wings of Time were fleet
As I gazed; and neither spoke, for we felt
    Life was so sweet!

And the odorous limes were dim above
  As we leant on a drooping bough;
And the darkling air was a breath of love,
  And a witching thrush sang "Now!"
For the sun dropt low, and the twilight grew
  As we listen'd and sigh'd, and leant;
That day was the sweetest day — and we knew
    What the sweetness meant.

THE CUCKOO.

WE heard it calling, clear and low,
That tender April morn; we stood
And listened in the quiet wood,
We heard it, ay, long years ago.

It came, and with a strange, sweet cry,
A friend, but from a far-off land;
We stood and listened, hand in hand,
And heart to heart, my Love and I.

In dreamland then we found our joy,
And so it seemed as 't were the Bird
That Helen in old times had heard
At noon beneath the oaks of Troy.

O time far off, and yet so near!
It came to her in that hush'd grove,
It warbled while the wooing throve,
It sang the song she loved to hear.

And now I hear its voice again,
    And still its message is of peace,
    It sings of love that will not cease—
For me it never sings in vain.

GERTRUDE'S NECKLACE.

AS Gertrude skipt from babe to girl,
Her Necklace lengthen'd, pearl by pearl;
Year after year it grew, and grew,
For every birthday gave her two.
Her neck is lovely, — soft and fair,
And now her Necklace glimmers there.

So cradled, let it fall and rise,
And all her graces symbolize.
Perchance this pearl, without a speck,
Once was as warm on Sappho's neck;
Where are the happy, twilight pearls
That braided Beatrice's curls?

Is Gerty loved? Is Gerty loth?
Or, if she 's either, is she both?
She 's fancy free, but sweeter far
Than many plighted maidens are:
Will Gerty smile us all away,
And still be Gerty? Who can say?

But let her wear her Precious Toy,
And I'll rejoice to see her joy:
Her bauble's only one degree
Less frail, less fugitive than we,
For time, ere long, will snap the skein,
And scatter all her Pearls again.

SAMUEL LOVER.

1797-1868

*THE ANGEL'S WHISPER.**

A BABY was sleeping,
Its mother was weeping,
For the husband was far on the wild raging Sea;
And the tempest was swelling
Round the fisherman's dwelling;
And she cried, "Dermot darling, oh come back to me!"

Her beads while she numbered,
The baby still slumbered,
And smiled in her face as she bended her knee;

* A superstition of great beauty prevails in Ireland that when a child smiles in its sleep it is "talking with angels."

"O blest be that warning,
My child thy sleep adorning,
For I know that the angels are whispering with thee!

"And while they are keeping
Bright watch o'er thy sleeping,
Oh, pray to them softly, my baby, with me!
And say thou wouldst rather
They'd watch o'er thy father;
For I know that the angels are whispering with thee!"

The dawn of the morning
Saw Dermot returning,
And the wife wept with joy her babe's father to see;
And closely caressing
Her child, with a blessing,
Said, "I knew that the angels were whispering with thee!"

WHAT WILL YOU DO, LOVE?

I.

"WHAT will you do, love, when I am going
With white sail flowing,
The seas beyond —
What will you do, love, when waves divide us,
And friends may chide us
For being fond?"
"Tho' waves divide us — and friends be chiding,
In faith abiding,
I 'll still be true!
And I 'll pray for thee on the stormy ocean,
In deep devotion —
That 's what I 'll do!"

II.

"What would you do, love, if distant tidings
Thy fond confidings
Should undermine? —

And I abiding 'neath sultry skies,
Should think other eyes
Were as bright as thine?"
"Oh, name it not:—tho' guilt and shame
Were on thy name
I 'd still be true:
But that heart of thine—should another share it—
I could not bear it!
What would I do?"

III.

"What would you do, love, when home returning
With hopes high burning,
With wealth for you,
If my bark, which bounded o'er foreign foam,
Should be lost near home—
Ah! what would you do?"—
"So thou wert spared—I 'd bless the morrow,
In want and sorrow,
That left me you;
And I 'd welcome thee from the wasting billow,
This heart thy pillow—
That 's what I 'd do!"

CHARLES MACKAY.

1814-1889

I LOVE MY LOVE.

I.

WHAT is the meaning of the song
 That rings so clear and loud,
Thou nightingale amid the copse —
 Thou lark above the cloud?
What says the song, thou joyous thrush,
 Up in the walnut-tree?
"I love my Love, because I know
 My Love loves me."

II.

What is the meaning of thy thought,
 O maiden fair and young?

There is such pleasure in thine eyes,
  Such music on thy tongue;
There is such glory on thy face —
  What can the meaning be?
"I love my Love, because I know
  My Love loves me."

III.

O happy words! at Beauty's feet
  We sing them ere our prime;
And when the early summers pass,
  And Care comes on with Time,
Still be it ours, in Care's despite,
  To join the chorus free —
"I love my Love, because I know
  My Love loves me."

O YE TEARS!

O YE tears! O ye tears! that have long refused to flow,
Ye are welcome to my heart,—thawing, thawing, like the snow;
I feel the hard clod soften, and the early snow-drop spring,
And the healing fountains gush, and the wildernesses sing.

O ye tears! O ye tears! I am thankful that ye run;
Though ye trickle in the darkness, ye shall glitter in the sun.
The rainbow cannot shine if the rain refuse to fall,
And the eyes that cannot weep are the saddest eyes of all.

O ye tears! O ye tears! till I felt you on my cheek,
I was selfish in my sorrow, I was stubborn, I was weak.

Ye have given me strength to conquer, and I stand
erect and free,
And know that I am human by the light of sympathy.

O ye tears! O ye tears! ye relieve me of my pain:
The barren rock of pride has been stricken once again;
Like the rock that Moses smote, amid Horeb's burning sand,
It yields the flowing water to make gladness in the
land.

There is light upon my path, there is sunshine in my
heart,
And the leaf and fruit of life shall not utterly depart.
Ye restore to me the freshness and the bloom of long
ago —
O ye tears! happy tears! I am thankful that ye flow!

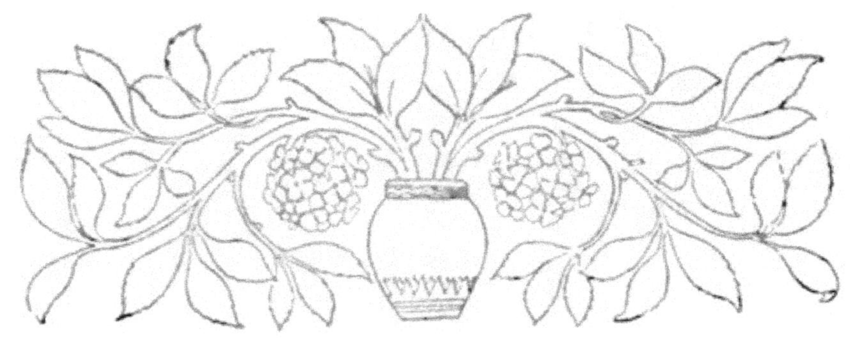

FRANCIS MAHONEY.

1805-1866.

THE BELLS OF SHANDON.

Sabbata pango;
Funera plango;
Solemnia clango.
— *Inscription on an old bell.*

WITH deep affection
And recollection
I often think of
Those Shandon bells,
Whose sounds so wild would,
In the days of childhood,
Fling round my cradle
Their magic spells.

On this I ponder
Where'er I wander,
And thus grow fonder,
Sweet Cork, of thee, —

With thy bells of Shandon,
That sound so grand on
The pleasant waters
  Of the river Lee.

I 've heard bells chiming
Full many a clime in,
Tolling sublime in
  Cathedral shrine,
While at a glibe rate
Brass tongues would vibrate;
But all their music
  Spoke naught like thine.

For memory, dwelling
On each proud swelling
Of thy belfry, knelling
  Its bold notes free,
Made the bells of Shandon
Sound far more grand on
The pleasant waters
  Of the river Lee.

I 've heard bells tolling
Old Adrian's Mole in,
Their thunder rolling
　From the Vatican,—
And cymbals glorious
Swinging uproarious
In the gorgeous turrets
　Of Notre Dame;

But thy sounds were sweeter
Than the dome of Peter
Flings o'er the Tiber,
　Pealing solemnly.
Oh! the bells of Shandon
Sound far more grand on
The pleasant waters
　Of the river Lee.

There 's a bell in Moscow;
While on tower and kiosk O
In St. Sophia
　The Turkman gets,

And loud in air
Calls men to prayer,
From the tapering summit
  Of tall minarets.

Such empty phantom
I freely grant them;
But there 's an anthem
  More dear to me, —
'T is the bells of Shandon,
That sound so grand on
The pleasant waters
  Of the river Lee.

GERALD MASSEY.

1828.

SONG.

ALL glorious as the Rainbow's birth,
  She came in Spring-tide's golden hours;
When Heaven went hand-in-hand with Earth,
  And May was crowned with buds and flowers!
The mounting devil at my heart
  Clomb faintlier as my life did win
The charmèd heaven, she wrought apart,
  To wake its slumbering Angel in!
With radiant mien she trod serene,
  And passed me smiling by!
O! who that looked could chance but love?
  Not I, sweet soul, not I.

The dewy eyelids of the Dawn
  Ne'er oped such heaven as hers can show:
It seemed her dear eyes might have shone
  As jewels in some starry brow.
Her face flashed glory like a shrine,
  Or lily-bell with sunburst bright;
Where came and went love-thoughts divine,
  As low winds walk the leaves in light:
She wore her beauty with the grace
  Of Summer's star-clad sky;
O! who that looked could help but love?
  Not I, sweet soul, not I.

Her budding breasts like fragrant fruit
  Of love were ripening to be pressed:
Her voice, that shook my heart's red root,
  Yet might not break a babe's soft rest!
More liquid than the running brooks,
  More vernal than the voice of Spring,
When Nightingales are in their nooks,
  And all the leafy thickets ring.

The love she coyly hid at heart
  Was shyly conscious in her eye;
O! who that looked could help but love?
  Not I, sweet soul, not I.

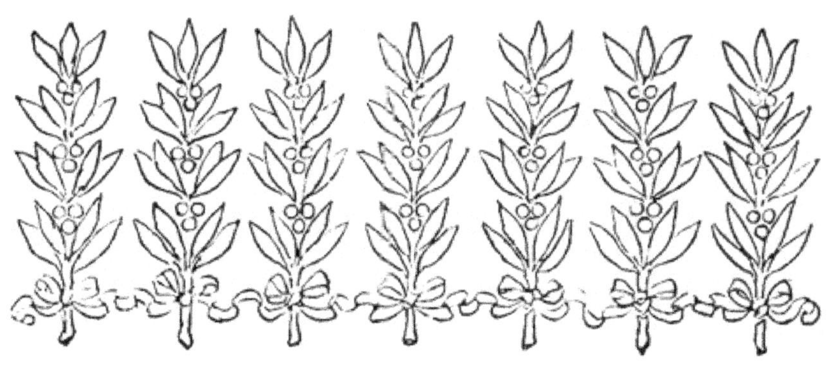

ARTHUR O'SHAUGHNESSY.

1844-1881.

A LOVE SYMPHONY.

ALONG the garden ways just now
  I heard the flowers speak;
The white rose told me of your brow,
  The red rose of your cheek;
The lily of your bended head,
  The bindweed of your hair:
Each looked its loveliest and said
    You were more fair.

I went into the wood anon,
  And heard the wild birds sing,
How sweet you were; they warbled on,
  Piped, trilled the self-same thing.

Thrush, blackbird, linnet, without pause,
  The burden did repeat,
And still began again because
    You were more sweet.

And then I went down to the sea,
  And heard it murmuring too,
Part of an ancient mystery,
  All made of me and you.
How many a thousand years ago
  I loved, and you were sweet—
Longer I could not stay, and so
  I fled back to your feet.

I MADE ANOTHER GARDEN.

I MADE another garden, yea,
  For my new love;
I left the dead rose where it lay,
  And set the new above.
Why did the summer not begin?
  Why did my heart not haste?
My old love came and walked therein,
  And laid the garden waste.

She entered with her weary smile,
  Just as of old;
She looked around a little while,
  And shivered at the cold.
Her passing touch was death to all,
  Her passing look a blight;
She made the white rose-petals fall,
  And turned the red rose white.

Her pale robe, clinging to the grass,
  Seemed like a snake
That bit the grass and ground, alas!
  And a sad trail did make.

She went up slowly to the gate;
  And there, just as of yore,
She turned back at the last to wait,
  And say farewell once more.

ADELAIDE ANNE PROCTER

1825–1864

THE LOST CHORD.

SEATED one day at the Organ,
  I was weary and ill at ease,
And my fingers wandered idly
  Over the noisy keys.

I do not know what I was playing,
  Or what I was dreaming then;
But I struck one chord of music,
  Like the sound of a great Amen.

It flooded the crimson twilight
  Like the close of an Angel's Psalm,
And it lay on my fevered spirit
  With a touch of infinite calm.

It quieted pain and sorrow,
  Like love overcoming strife;
It seemed the harmonious echo
  From our discordant Life.

It linked all perplexèd meanings
  Into one perfect peace,
And trembled away into silence
  As if it were loth to cease.

I have sought, but I seek it vainly,
  That one lost chord divine,
Which came from the soul of the Organ,
  And entered into mine.

It may be that Death's bright angel
  Will speak in that chord again,—
It may be that only in Heaven
  I shall hear that grand Amen.

SENT TO HEAVEN.

I HAD a Message to send her,
To her whom my soul loved best;
But I had my task to finish,
And she was gone home to rest.

To rest in the far bright heaven;
Oh, so far away from here,
It was vain to speak to my darling,
For I knew she could not hear!

I had a message to send her,
So tender, and true, and sweet,
I longed for an Angel to bear it,
And lay it down at her feet.

I placed it, one summer evening,
On a Cloudlet's fleecy breast;
But it faded in golden splendour,
And died in the crimson west.

I gave it the Lark next morning,
And I watched it soar and soar;
But its pinions grew faint and weary,
And it fluttered to earth once more.

To the heart of a Rose I told it;
And the perfume, sweet and rare,
Growing faint on the blue bright ether,
Was lost in the balmy air.

I laid it upon a Censer,
And I saw the incense rise;
But its clouds of rolling silver
Could not reach the far blue skies.

I cried, in my passionate longing:—
"Has the earth no Angel-friend
Who will carry my love the message
That my heart desires to send?"

Then I heard a strain of music,
So mighty, so pure, so clear,
That my very sorrow was silent,
And my heart stood still to hear.

And I felt, in my soul's deep yearning,
  At last the sure answer stir:—
"The music will go up to Heaven,
  And carry my thought to her."

It rose in harmonious rushing
  Of mingled voices and strings,
And I tenderly laid my message
  On the Music's outspread wings.

I heard it float farther and farther,
  In sound more perfect than speech;
Farther than sight can follow,
  Farther than soul can reach.

And I know that at last my message
  Has passed through the golden gate:
So my heart is no longer restless,
  And I am content to wait.

B. W. PROCTER (BARRY CORNWALL).

1787-1874.

THE POET'S SONG TO HIS WIFE.

SET TO MUSIC BY THE CHEVALIER NEUKOMM.

HOW many Summers, love,
  Have I been thine?
How many days, thou dove,
  Hast thou been mine?
Time, like the wingèd wind
  When 't bends the flowers,
Hath left no mark behind,
  To count the hours!

Some weight of thought, though loth,
  On thee he leaves;
Some lines of care round both
  Perhaps he weaves;

Some fears, — a soft regret
  For joys scarce known;
Sweet looks we half forget; —
  All else is flown!

Ah! with what thankless heart
  I mourn and sing!
Look, where our children start,
  Like sudden Spring!
With tongues all sweet and low,
  Like a pleasant rhyme,
They tell how much I owe
  To thee and Time!

A PETITION TO TIME.

1831.

TOUCH us gently, Time!
  Let us glide adown thy stream
Gently, — as we sometimes glide
  Through a quiet dream!
Humble voyagers are We,
Husband, wife, and children three —
(One is lost, — an angel, fled
To the azure overhead!)

Touch us gently, Time!
  We 've not proud nor soaring wings:
Our ambition, *our* content
  Lies in simple things.
Humble voyagers are We,
O'er Life's dim unsounded sea,
Seeking only some calm clime: —
Touch us *gently*, gentle Time!

A BACCHANALIAN SONG.

SET TO MUSIC BY MR. H. PHILLIPS.

SING!—Who sings
To her who weareth a hundred rings?
Ah, who is this lady fine?
The VINE, boys, the VINE!
The mother of mighty Wine.
A roamer is she
O'er wall and tree,
And sometimes very good company.

Drink!—Who drinks
To her who blusheth and never thinks?
Ah, who is this maid of thine?
The GRAPE, boys, the GRAPE!
O, never let her escape
Until she be turned to Wine!
For better is she
Than vine can be,
And very, very good company!

Dream! — Who dreams
Of the God that governs a thousand streams?
  Ah, who is this Spirit fine?
  'T is WINE, boys, 't is WINE!
  God Bacchus, a friend of mine.
    O better is he
    Than grape or tree,
And the best of all good company.

SHE WAS NOT FAIR NOR FULL OF GRACE.

SHE was not fair, nor full of grace,
  Nor crowned with thought or aught beside;
No wealth had she, of mind or face,
  To win our love, or raise our pride:
No lover's thought her cheek did touch;
  No poet's dream was 'round her thrown;
And yet we miss her—ah, too much,
  Now—she hath flown!

We miss her when the morning calls,
  As one that mingled in our mirth;
We miss her when the evening falls,—
  A trifle wanted on the earth!
Some fancy small or subtle thought
  Is checked ere to its blossom grown;
Some chain is broken that we wrought,
  Now—she hath flown!

No solid good, nor hope defined,
  Is marred now she hath sunk in night;

And yet the strong immortal Mind
  Is stopped in its triumphant flight!
Stern friend, what power is in a tear,
  What strength in one poor thought alone,
When all we know is — "She was here,"
  And — "She hath flown!"

THE SEA-KING.

SET TO MUSIC BY THE CHEVALIER NEUKOMM.

COME sing, Come sing, of the great Sea-King,
And the fame that now hangs o'er him,
Who once did sweep o'er the vanquish'd deep,
And drove the world before him!
His deck was a throne, on the ocean lone,
And the sea was his park of pleasure,
Where he scattered in fear the human deer,
And rested,—when he had leisure!
Come,—shout and sing
Of the great Sea-King,
And ride in the track he rode in!
He sits at the head
Of the mighty dead,
On the red right hand of Odin!

He sprang, from birth, like a God on earth,
And soared on his victor pinions,
And he traversed the sea, as the eagles flee,
When they gaze on their blue dominions.

His whole earth life was a conquering strife,
And he lived till his beard grew hoary,
And he died at last, by his blood-red mast,
And now—he is lost in glory!
So,—shout and sing, &c.

A SERENADE.

SET TO MUSIC BY THE CHEVALIER NEUKOMM.

AWAKE!—The starry midnight Hour
Hangs charmed, and pauseth in its flight:
In its own sweetness sleeps the flower;
And the doves lie hushed in deep delight!
Awake! Awake!
Look forth, my love, for Love's sweet sake!

Awake!—Soft dews will soon arise
From daisied mead, and thorny brake;
Then, Sweet, uncloud those eastern eyes,
And like the tender morning break!
Awake! Awake!
Dawn forth, my love, for Love's sweet sake!

Awake!—Within the musk-rose bower
I watch, pale flower of love, for thee;
Ah, come, and shew the starry Hour
What wealth of love thou hid'st from me!
Awake! Awake!
Shew all thy love, for Love's sweet sake!

Awake! — Ne'er heed, though listening Night
  Steal music from thy silver voice:
Uncloud thy beauty, rare and bright,
  And bid the world and me rejoice!
      Awake! Awake!
      She comes, — at last, for Love's sweet sake!

KING DEATH.

SET TO MUSIC BY THE CHEVALIER NEUKOMM.

KING DEATH was a rare old fellow!
He sate where no sun could shine;
And he lifted his hand so yellow,
And poured out his coal-black wine.
Hurrah! for the coal-black Wine!

There came to him many a Maiden,
Whose eyes had forgot to shine;
And Widows, with grief o'erladen,
For a draught of his sleepy wine.
Hurrah! for the coal-black Wine!

The Scholar left all his learning;
The Poet his fancied woes;
And the Beauty her bloom returning,
As the beads of the black wine rose.
Hurrah! for the coal-black Wine!

All came to the royal old fellow,
  Who laughed till his eyes dropped brine,
As he gave them his hand so yellow,
  And pledged them in Death's black wine.
        Hurrah! — Hurrah!
        Hurrah! for the coal-black Wine!

SIT DOWN, SAD SOUL.

SIT down, sad soul, and count
The moments flying:
Come,—tell the sweet amount
That 's lost by sighing!
How many smiles?—a score?
Then laugh, and count no more;
For day is dying!

Lie down, sad soul, and sleep,
And no more measure
The flight of Time, nor weep
The loss of leisure;
But here, by this lone stream,
Lie down with us, and dream
Of starry treasure!

We dream: do thou the same:
We love—for ever:

We laugh; yet few we shame,
 The gentle, never.
Stay, then, till Sorrow dies;
Then — hope and happy skies
  Are thine for ever!

A DRINKING SONG.

DRINK, and fill the night with mirth!
  Let us have a mighty measure,
Till we quite forget the earth,
  And soar into the world of pleasure.
Drink, and let a health go round,
  ('T is the drinker's noble duty,)
To the eyes that shine and wound,
  To the mouths that bud in beauty!

Here 's to Helen! Why, ah! why
  Doth she fly from my pursuing?
Here 's to Marian, cold and shy!
  May she warm before thy wooing!
Here 's to Janet! I 've been e'er,
  Boy and man, her staunch defender,
Always sworn that she was fair,
  Always *known* that she was tender!

Fill the deep-mouthed glasses high!
  Let them with the champagne tremble,

Like the loose wrack in the sky,
  When the four wild winds assemble!
Here 's to all the love on earth,
  (Love, the young man's, wise man's treasure!)
Drink, and fill your throats with mirth!
  Drink, and drown the world in pleasure!

PEACE! WHAT DO TEARS AVAIL?

PEACE! what can tears avail?
She lies all dumb and pale,
And from her eye,
The spirit of lovely life is fading,
And she must die!
Why looks the lover wroth? the friend upbraiding?
Reply, reply!

Hath she not dwelt too long
'Midst pain, and grief, and wrong?
Then, why not die?
Why suffer again her doom of sorrow,
And hopeless lie?
Why nurse the trembling dream until to-morrow?
Reply, reply!

Death! Take her to thine arms,
In all her stainless charms,

And with her fly
To heavenly haunts, where, clad in brightness,
The Angels lie!
Wilt bear her there, O Death! in all her whiteness?
Reply, — reply!

THE SEA.

SET TO MUSIC BY THE CHEVALIER NEUKOMM.

THE Sea! the Sea! the open Sea!
The blue, the fresh, the ever free!
Without a mark, without a bound,
It runneth the earth's wide regions 'round;
It plays with the clouds; it mocks the skies;
Or like a cradled creature lies.

I 'm on the Sea! I 'm on the Sea!
I am where I would ever be;
With the blue above, and the blue below,
And silence wheresoe'er I go;
If a storm should come and awake the deep,
What matter? *I* shall ride and sleep.

I love (oh! *how* I love) to ride
On the fierce foaming bursting tide,
When every mad wave drowns the moon,
Or whistles aloft his tempest tune,

And tells how goeth the world below,
And why the south-west blasts do blow.

I never was on the dull tame shore,
But I loved the great Sea more and more,
And backwards flew to her billowy breast,
Like a bird that seeketh its mother's nest;
And a mother she *was*, and *is* to me;
For I was born on the open Sea!

The waves were white, and red the morn,
In the noisy hour when I was born;
And the whale it whistled, the porpoise rolled,
And the dolphins bared their backs of gold;
And never was heard such an outcry wild
As welcomed to life the Ocean-child!

I've lived since then, in calm and strife,
Full fifty summers a sailor's life,
With wealth to spend and a power to range,
But never have sought, nor sighed for change;
And Death, whenever he come to me,
Shall come on the wild unbounded Sea!

CHRISTINA G. ROSSETTI.

1830-1895

SONG.

WHEN I am dead, my dearest,
 Sing no sad songs for me;
Plant thou no roses at my head,
 Nor shady cypress-tree:
Be the green grass above me
 With showers and dewdrops wet;
And if thou wilt, remember,
 And if thou wilt, forget.

I shall not see the shadows,
 I shall not feel the rain;
I shall not hear the nightingale
 Sing on, as if in pain:

And dreaming through the twilight
  That doth not rise nor set,
Haply I may remember,
  And haply may forget.

SONG.

O ROSES for the flush of youth,
And laurel for the perfect prime;
But pluck an ivy branch for me
Grown old before my time.

O violets for the grave of youth,
And bay for those dead in their prime;
Give me the withered leaves I chose
Before in the old time.

SONG.

TWO doves upon the selfsame branch,
  Two lilies on a single stem,
Two butterflies upon one flower:—
  O happy they who look on them.

Who look upon them hand in hand
  Flushed in the rosy summer light;
Who look upon them hand in hand
  And never give a thought to night.

THREE SEASONS.

"A CUP for hope!" she said,
In springtime ere the bloom was old:
The crimson wine was poor and cold
By her mouth's richer red.

"A cup for love!" how low,
How soft the words; and all the while
Her blush was rippling with a smile
Like summer after snow.

"A cup for memory!"
Cold cup that one must drain alone:
While autumn winds are up and moan
Across the barren sea.

Hope, memory, love:
Hope for fair morn, and love for day,
And memory for the evening gray
And solitary dove.

DANTE GABRIEL ROSSETTI.

1828-1882.

A LITTLE WHILE.

A LITTLE while a little love
The hour yet bears for thee and me
Who have not drawn the veil to see
If still our heaven be lit above.
Thou merely, at the day's last sigh,
Hast felt thy soul prolong the tone;
And I have heard the night-wind cry
And deemed its speech mine own.

A little while a little love
The scattering autumn hoards for us
Whose bower is not yet ruinous
Nor quite unleaved our songless grove.

Only across the shaken boughs
  We hear the flood-tides seek the sea,
And deep in both our hearts they rouse
    One wail for thee and me.

A little while a little love
  May yet be ours who have not said
  The word it makes our eyes afraid
To know that each is thinking of.
Not yet the end: be our lips dumb
  In smiles a little season yet:
I'll tell thee, when the end is come,
    How we may best forget.

SUDDEN LIGHT.

I HAVE been here before,
But when or how I cannot tell:
I know the grass beyond the door,
The sweet keen smell,
The sighing sound, the lights around the shore.

You have been mine before,—
How long ago I may not know:
But just when at that swallow's soar
Your neck turned so,
Some veil did fall,—I knew it all of yore.

Has this been thus before?
And shall not thus time's eddying flight
Still with our lives our loves restore
In death's despite,
And day and night yield one delight once more?

THREE SHADOWS.

I LOOKED and saw your eyes
  In the shadow of your hair,
As a traveller sees the stream
  In the shadow of the wood;
And I said, "My faint heart sighs,
  Ah me! to linger there,
To drink deep and to dream
  In that sweet solitude."

I looked and saw your heart
  In the shadow of your eyes,
As a seeker sees the gold
  In the shadow of the stream;
And I said, "Ah, me! what art
  Should win the immortal prize,
Whose want must make life cold
  And Heaven a hollow dream?"

I looked and saw your love
  In the shadow of your heart,
As a diver sees the pearl
  In the shadow of the sea;
And I murmured, not above
  My breath, but all apart, —
"Ah! you can love, true girl,
  And is your love for me?"

WILLIAM BELL SCOTT.

1812–1890.

PARTING AND MEETING AGAIN.

LAST time I parted from my Dear
The linnet sang from the briar-bush,
The throstle from the dell;
The stream too carolled full and clear.
It was the spring-time of the year,
And both the linnet and the thrush
I love them well
Since last I parted from my Dear.

But when he came again to me
The barley rustled high and low,

Linnet and thrush were still;
Yellowed the apple on the tree,
'T was autumn merry as it could be,
What time the white ships come and go
Under the hill;
They brought him back again to me,
Brought him safely o'er the sea.

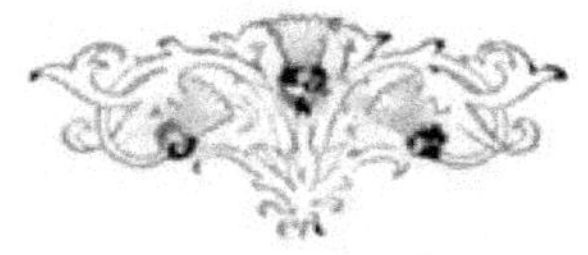

JOSEPH SKIPSEY.

1832

A MERRY BEE.

A GOLDEN bee a-cometh
  O'er the mere, glassy mere,
And a merry tale he hummeth
    In my ear.

How he seized and kist a blossom,
  From its tree, thorny tree,
Plucked and placed in Annie's bosom,
    Hums the bee!

THE SONGSTRESS.

BACK flies my soul to other years,
When thou that charming lay repeatest,
When smiles were only chased by tears,
Yet sweeter far than smiles the sweetest.

Thy music ends, and where are they?
Those golden times by memory cherished?
O, Syren, sing no more that lay,
Or sing till I like them have perished!

THE VIOLET AND THE ROSE.

THE Violet invited my kiss,—
I kissed it and called it my bride;
"Was ever one slighted like this?"
Sighed the Rose as it stood by my side.

My heart ever open to grief,
To comfort the fair one I turned;
"Of fickle ones thou art the chief!"
Frowned the Violet, and pouted and mourned.

Then, to end all disputes, I entwined
The love-stricken blossoms in one;
But that instant their beauty declined,
And I wept for the deed I had done!

J. ASHBY STERRY.

REGRETS.

I.

O FOR the look of those pure grey eyes—
Seeming to plead and speak—
The parted lips and the deep-drawn sighs,
The blush on the kissen cheek!

II.

O for the tangle of soft brown hair,
Lazily blown by the breeze;
The fleeting hours unshadowed by care,
Shaded by tremulous trees!

III.

O for the dream of those sunny days,
With their bright unbroken spell,
And the thrilling sweet untutored praise—
From the lips once loved so well!

IV.

O for the feeling of days agone,
  The simple faith and the truth,
The spring of time and life's rosy dawn—
  O for the love and the youth!

DAISY'S DIMPLES.

I.

LITTLE dimples so sweet and soft,
  Love the cheek of my love:
The mark of Cupid's dainty hand,
  Before he wore a glove.

II.

Laughing dimples of tender love
  Smile on my darling's cheek;
Sweet hallowed spots where kisses lurk,
  And play at hide and seek.

III.

Fain would I hide my kisses there
  At morning's rosy light,
To come and seek them back again
  In silver hush of night.

A LOVER'S LULLABY.

I.

MIRROR your sweet eyes in mine, love,
See how they glitter and shine!
Quick fly such moments divine, love,
Link your lithe fingers in mine!

II.

Lay your soft cheek against mine, love,
Pillow your head on my breast;
While your brown locks I entwine, love,
Pout your red lips when they 're prest!

III.

Mirror your fate, then, in mine, love;
Sorrow and sighing resign:
Life is too short to repine, love,
Link your fair future in mine!

ALGERNON CHARLES SWINBURNE.

1837.

A MATCH.

IF love were what the rose is,
　And I were like the leaf,
Our lives would grow together
In sad or singing weather,
Blown fields or flowerful closes,
　Green pleasure or grey grief;
If love were what the rose is,
　And I were like the leaf.

If I were what the words are,
　And love were like the tune,
With double sound or single
Delight our lips would mingle,

With kisses glad as birds are
  That get sweet rain at noon;
If I were what the words are,
  And love were like the tune.

If you were life, my darling,
  And I your love were death,
We 'd shine and snow together
Ere March made sweet the weather
With daffodil and starling
  And hours of fruitful breath;
If you were life, my darling,
  And I your love were death.

If you were thrall to sorrow,
  And I were page to joy,
We 'd play for lives and seasons
With loving looks and treasons
And tears of night and morrow
  And laughs of maid and boy;
If you were thrall to sorrow,
  And I were page to joy.

If you were April's lady,
  And I were lord in May,
We'd throw with leaves for hours
And draw for days with flowers,
Till day like night were shady
  And night were bright like day;
If you were April's lady,
  And I were lord in May.

If you were queen of pleasure,
  And I were king of pain,
We'd hunt down love together,
Pluck out his flying-feather,
And teach his feet a measure,
  And find his mouth a rein;
If you were queen of pleasure,
  And I were king of pain.

RONDEL.

KISSING her hair I sat against her feet,
Wove and unwove it, wound and found it sweet;
Made fast therewith her hands, drew down her eyes,
Deep as deep flowers and dreamy like dim skies;
With her own tresses bound and found her fair,
Kissing her hair.

Sleep were no sweeter than her face to me,
Sleep of cold sea-bloom under the cold sea;
What pain could get between my face and hers?
What new sweet thing would love not relish worse?
Unless, perhaps, white death had kissed me there,
Kissing her hair?

SONG.

FROM "FELISE."

O LIPS that mine have grown into
  Like April's kissing May,
O fervent eyelids letting through
Those eyes the greenest of things blue,
  The bluest of things gray,

If you were I and I were you,
  How could I love you, say?
How could the roseleaf love the rue,
The day love nightfall and her dew,
  Though night may love the day?

ALFRED TENNYSON.

1809–1892.

THE BUGLE SONG.

FROM "THE PRINCESS."

THE splendour falls on castle walls
And snowy summits old in story:
The long light shakes across the lakes,
And the wild cataract leaps in glory.
Blow, bugle, blow, set the wild echoes flying,
Blow, bugle; answer, echoes, dying, dying, dying.

O hark, O hear! how thin and clear,
And thinner, clearer, farther going!

O sweet and far from cliff and scar
  The horns of Elfland faintly blowing!
Blow, let us hear the purple glens replying:
Blow, bugle; answer, echoes, dying, dying, dying.

O love, they die in yon rich sky,
  They faint on hill or field or river:
Our echoes roll from soul to soul,
  And grow for ever and for ever.
Blow, bugle, blow, set the wild echoes flying,
And answer, echoes, answer, dying, dying, dying.

BREAK, BREAK, BREAK.

BREAK, break, break,
  On thy cold gray stones, O Sea!
And I would that my tongue could utter
  The thoughts that arise in me.

O well for the fisherman's boy,
  That he shouts with his sister at play!
O well for the sailor lad,
  That he sings in his boat on the bay!

And the stately ships go on
  To their haven under the hill;
But O for the touch of a vanished hand,
  And the sound of a voice that is still!

Break, break, break,
  At the foot of thy crags, O Sea!
But the tender grace of a day that is dead
  Will never come back to me.

TEARS, IDLE TEARS.

FROM "THE PRINCESS."

TEARS, idle tears, I know not what they mean,
  Tears from the depth of some divine despair
Rise in the heart, and gather to the eyes,
In looking on the happy Autumn-fields,
And thinking of the days that are no more.

Fresh as the first beam glittering on a sail,
That brings our friends up from the underworld,
Sad as the last which reddens over one
That sinks with all we love below the verge;
So sad, so fresh, the days that are no more.

Ah, sad and strange as in dark summer dawns
The earliest pipe of half-awakened birds
To dying ears, when unto dying eyes
The casement slowly grows a glimmering square;
So sad, so strange, the days that are no more.

Dear as remembered kisses after death,
And sweet as those by hopeless fancy feigned
On lips that are for others; deep as love,
Deep as first love, and wild with all regret;
O Death in Life, the days that are no more.

SWEET AND LOW.

FROM "THE PRINCESS."

SWEET and low, sweet and low,
  Wind of the western sea,
Low, low, breathe and blow,
  Wind of the western sea!
Over the rolling waters go,
Come from the dying moon, and blow,
  Blow him again to me;
While my little one, while my pretty one, sleeps.

Sleep and rest, sleep and rest,
  Father will come to thee soon;
Rest, rest, on mother's breast,
  Father will come to thee soon;
Father will come to his babe in the nest,
Silver sails all out of the west
  Under the silver moon:
Sleep, my little one, sleep, my pretty one, sleep.

TURN, FORTUNE, TURN THY WHEEL.

FROM "THE MARRIAGE OF GERAINT."

TURN, Fortune, turn thy wheel and lower the proud;
Turn thy wild wheel thro' sunshine, storm, and cloud;
Thy wheel and thee we neither love nor hate.

Turn, Fortune, turn thy wheel with smile or frown;
With that wild wheel we go not up or down;
Our hoard is little, but our hearts are great.

Smile and we smile, the lords of many lands;
Frown and we smile, the lords of our own hands;
For man is man and master of his fate.

Turn, turn thy wheel above the staring crowd;
Thy wheel and thou are shadows in the cloud;
Thy wheel and thee we neither love nor hate.

VIVIEN'S SONG.

FROM "MERLIN AND VIVIEN."

IN Love, if Love be Love, if Love be ours,
Faith and unfaith can ne'er be equal powers:
Unfaith in aught is want of faith in all.

It is the little rift within the lute,
That by and by will make the music mute,
And ever widening slowly silence all.

The little rift within the lover's lute
Or little pitted speck in garnered fruit,
That rotting inward slowly moulders all.

It is not worth the keeping: let it go:
But shall it? answer, darling, answer, no.
And trust me not at all or all in all.

WILLIAM MAKEPEACE THACKERAY.

1811-1863.

AT THE CHURCH GATE.

FROM "PENDENNIS."

ALTHOUGH I enter not,
Yet round about the spot
Ofttimes I hover:
And near the sacred gate,
With longing eyes I wait,
Expectant of her.

The Minster bell tolls out
Above the city's rout,
And noise and humming:
They've hushed the Minster bell:
The organ 'gins to swell:
She's coming, she's coming!

My lady comes at last,
Timid, and stepping fast,
  And hastening hither,
With modest eyes downcast:
She comes — she 's here — she 's past —
  May heaven go with her!

Kneel, undisturbed, fair saint!
Pour out your praise or plaint
  Meekly and duly;
I will not enter there,
To sully your pure prayer
  With thoughts unruly.

But suffer me to pace
Round the forbidden place,
  Lingering a minute;
Like outcast spirits who wait
And see through heaven's gate
  Angels within it.

THE MAHOGANY TREE.

CHRISTMAS is here;
Winds whistle shrill,
Icy and chill,
Little care we:
Little we fear
Weather without
Sheltered about
The Mahogany Tree.

Once on the boughs
Birds of rare plume
Sang, in its bloom;
Night-birds are we:
Here we carouse,
Singing like them,
Perched round the stem
Of the jolly old tree.

Here let us sport,
Boys, as we sit;

Laughter and wit
Flashing so free.
Life is but short —
When we are gone,
Let them sing on,
Round the old tree.

Evenings we knew,
Happy as this;
Faces we miss,
Pleasant to see.
Kind hearts and true,
Gentle and just,
Peace to your dust!
We sing round the tree.

Care, like a dun,
Lurks at the gate:
Let the dog wait;
Happy we'll be!
Drink, every one;
Pile up the coals,
Fill the red bowls,
Round the old tree.

Drain we the cup.—
Friend, art afraid?
Spirits are laid
In the Red Sea.
Mantle it up;
Empty it yet;
Let us forget,
Round the old tree.

Sorrows, begone!
Life and its ills,
Duns and their bills,
Bid we to flee.
Come with the dawn,
Blue-devil sprite,
Leave us to-night,
Round the old tree.

GEORGE WALTER THORNBURY.

1828-1876.

DAYRISE AND SUNSET.

WHEN Spring casts all her swallows forth
Into the blue and lambent air,
When lilacs toss their purple plumes
And every cherry-tree grows fair,—
Through fields with morning tints a-glow
I take my rod and singing go.

Where lilies float on broad green leaves
Below the ripples of the mill,
When the white moth is hovering
In the dim sky so hushed and still,
I watch beneath the pollard ash
The greedy trout leap up and splash.

Or down where golden water flowers
  Are wading in the shallow tide,
While still the dusk is tinged with rose
  Like a brown cheek o'erflushed with pride —
I throw the crafty fly and wait;
Watching the big trout eye the bait.

It is the lover's twilight-time,
  And there 's a magic in the hour,
But I forget the sweets of love
  And all love's tyranny and power,
And with my feather-hidden steel
Sigh but to fill my woven creel.

Then upward darkling through the copse
  I push my eager homeward way,
Through glades of drowsy violets
  That never see the golden day.
Yes! while the night comes soft and slow
I take my rod and singing go.

THE THREE TROOPERS.

DURING THE PROTECTORATE.

INTO the Devil tavern
  Three booted troopers strode,
From spur to feather spotted and splashed
  With the mud of a winter road.
In each of their cups they dropped a crust,
  And stared at the guests with a frown;
Then drew their swords, and roared for a toast,
  "God send this Crum-well-down!"

A blue smoke rose from their pistol locks,
  Their sword blades were still wet;
There were long red smears on their jerkins of buff,
  As the table they overset.
Then into their cups they stirred the crusts,
  And cursed old London town;
They waved their swords, and drank with a stamp,
  "God send this Crum-well-down!"

The 'prentice dropped his can of beer,
  The host turned pale as a clout;
The ruby nose of the toping squires
  Grew white at the wild men's shout.
Then into their cups they flung their crusts,
  And shewed their teeth with a frown;
They flashed their swords as they gave the toast,
  "God send this Crum-well-down!"

The gambler dropped his dog's-ear'd cards,
  The waiting-women screamed,
As the light of the fire, like stains of blood,
  On the wild men's sabres gleamed.
Then into their cups they splashed their crusts,
  And cursed the fool of a town,
And leapt on the table, and roared a toast,
  "God send this Crum-well-down!"

Till on a sudden fire-bells rang,
  And the troopers sprang to horse;
The eldest muttered between his teeth,
  Hot curses—deep and coarse.

In their stirrup cups they flung the crusts,
  And cried as they spurred through the town,
With their keen swords drawn and their pistols cocked,
  "God send this Crum-well-down!"

Away they dashed through Temple Bar,
  Their red cloaks flowing free,
Their scabbards clashed, each back-piece shone —
  None liked to touch the three.
The silver cups that held the crusts
  They flung to the startled town,
Shouting again, with a blaze of swords,
  "God send this Crum-well-down!"

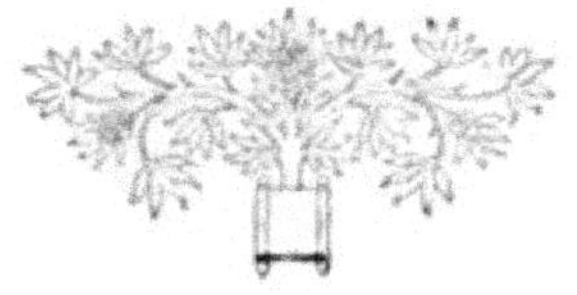

THE CUCKOO.

WHEN a warm and scented steam
Rises from the flowering earth;
When the green leaves are all still,
And the song birds cease their mirth;
In the silence before rain
Comes the cuckoo back again.

When the Spring is all but gone—
Tearful April, laughing May—
When a hush comes on the woods,
And the sunbeams cease to play;
In the silence before rain
Comes the cuckoo back again.

www.ingramcontent.com/pod-product-compliance
Lightning Source LLC
Chambersburg PA
CBHW030346270326
41926CB00009B/980
* 9 7 8 3 7 4 4 7 7 4 4 4 4 *